Chinese Minorities at Home and Abroad

The classification of ethnic identities (minzu) remains controversial in China. Categories established in the 1950s are still used by the state to administer minority areas, despite the existence of a complicated web of subjective identities which potentially undermines efforts to use these categories effectively.

This book offers a new, and sometimes unusual, perspective on ethnic relations in China, and on the interactions between China and other cultures. Two major themes run through the book: the classification of ethnic minorities in China by the state, and the implications of this practice; and the way in which China and the Chinese are seen by outsiders as well as insiders. The contributors, whose research is all based on fieldwork with the relevant communities, are from a wide range of backgrounds and are currently based in China, Hong Kong, Malaysia, Kazakhstan, and Germany. The subjects of their research are the politics of minority classification in the People's Republic of China; questions of identity in Xinjiang; Kazakhstani perceptions of China and the Chinese; Chinese Muslims in Malaysia; and the growing Chinese diaspora in Africa.

This book was originally published as a special issue of *Ethnic and Racial Studies*.

Michael Dillon is an independent China scholar specialising in the history, politics, and society of China. He was the founding Director of the Centre for Contemporary Chinese Studies at the University of Durham, UK; is a Fellow of the Royal Historical Society and the Royal Asiatic Society; and is a member of the Royal Institute of International Affairs (Chatham House).

Ethnic and Racial Studies

Series editors: Martin Bulmer, *University of Surrey, UK*, and John Solomos, *University of Warwick, UK*

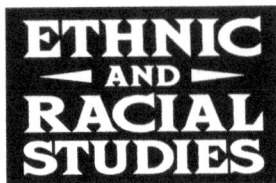

ETHNIC AND RACIAL STUDIES

The journal *Ethnic and Racial Studies* was founded in 1978 by John Stone to provide an international forum for high quality research on race, ethnicity, nationalism and ethnic conflict. At the time the study of race and ethnicity was still a relatively marginal sub-field of sociology, anthropology and political science. In the intervening period the journal has provided a space for the discussion of core theoretical issues, key developments and trends, and for the dissemination of the latest empirical research.

It is now the leading journal in its field and has helped to shape the development of scholarly research agendas. *Ethnic and Racial Studies* attracts submissions from scholars in a diverse range of countries and fields of scholarship, and crosses disciplinary boundaries. It is now available in both printed and electronic form. From 2015 it will publish 15 issues per year, three of which will be dedicated to *Ethnic and Racial Studies Review* offering expert guidance to the latest research through the publication of book reviews, symposia and discussion pieces, including reviews of work in languages other than English.

The Ethnic and Racial Studies book series contains a wide range of the journal's special issues. These special issues are an important contribution to the work of the journal, where leading social science academics bring together articles on specific themes and issues that are linked to the broad intellectual concerns of *Ethnic and Racial Studies*. The series editors work closely with the guest editors of the special issues to ensure that they meet the highest quality standards possible. Through publishing these special issues as a series of books, we hope to allow a wider audience of both scholars and students from across the social science disciplines to engage with the work of *Ethnic and Racial Studies*.

Most recent titles in the series include:

Minority Politics in the Middle East and North Africa
Edited by Will Kymlicka and Eva Pföstl

Muslims, Migration and Citizenship Processes of Inclusion and Exclusion
Edited by Martin Bulmer and John Solomos

Re-configuring Anti-racism
Edited by Yin Paradies

The Impact of Diasporas: Markers of Identity
Edited by Joanna Story and Iain Walker

Chinese Minorities at Home and Abroad
Edited by Michael Dillon

Intersectionality and Ethnic Entrepreneurship
Edited by Zulema Valdez and Mary Romero

Chinese Minorities at Home and Abroad

Edited by
Michael Dillon

Routledge
Taylor & Francis Group

LONDON AND NEW YORK

ETHNIC AND RACIAL STUDIES

First published 2017 by Routledge

2 Park Square, Milton Park, Abingdon, Oxfordshire OX14 4RN
52 Vanderbilt Avenue, New York, NY 10017

Routledge is an imprint of the Taylor & Francis Group, an informa business

First issued in paperback 2018

British Library Cataloguing in Publication Data
A catalogue record for this book is available from the British Library

ISBN 13: 978-0-415-78857-1 (hbk)
ISBN 13: 978-0-367-14295-7 (pbk)

Typeset in Myriad Pro
by RefineCatch Limited, Bungay, Suffolk

Publisher's Note
The publisher accepts responsibility for any inconsistencies that may have
arisen during the conversion of this book from journal articles to book chapters,
namely the possible inclusion of journal terminology.

Disclaimer
Every effort has been made to contact copyright holders for their permission to
reprint material in this book. The publishers would be grateful to hear from any
copyright holder who is not here acknowledged and will undertake to rectify
any errors or omissions in future editions of this book.

Contents

Citation Information   ix
Notes on Contributors   xi

Majorities and minorities in China: an introduction   1
Michael Dillon

1. Representation of ethnic minorities in socialist China   13
   Ke Fan

2. More Islamic, no less Chinese: explorations into overseas
   Chinese Muslim identities in Malaysia   30
   Chow Bing Ngeow and Hailong Ma

3. Kazakh perspective on China, the Chinese, and Chinese migration   51
   Aziz Burkhanov and Yu-Wen Chen

4. The discourse of racialization of labour and Chinese enterprises
   in Africa   71
   Barry Sautman and Yan Hairong

5. Socioeconomic attainment, cultural tastes, and ethnic identity:
   class subjectivities among Uyghurs in Ürümchi   91
   Xiaowei Zang

6. Blurring boundaries and negotiating subjectivities – the
   Uyghurized Han of southern Xinjiang, China   109
   Agnieszka Joniak-Lüthi

Index   127

Citation Information

The chapters in this book were originally published in *Ethnic and Racial Studies*, volume 39, issue 11–12 (September–October 2016). When citing this material, please use the original page numbering for each article, as follows:

Introduction
Majorities and minorities in China: an introduction
Michael Dillon
Ethnic and Racial Studies, volume 39, issue 11–12 (September–October 2016), pp. 2079–2090

Chapter 1
Representation of ethnic minorities in socialist China
Ke Fan
Ethnic and Racial Studies, volume 39, issue 11–12 (September–October 2016), pp. 2091–2107

Chapter 2
More Islamic, no less Chinese: explorations into overseas Chinese Muslim identities in Malaysia
Chow Bing Ngeow and Hailong Ma
Ethnic and Racial Studies, volume 39, issue 11–12 (September–October 2016), pp. 2108–2128

Chapter 3
Kazakh perspective on China, the Chinese, and Chinese migration
Aziz Burkhanov and Yu-Wen Chen
Ethnic and Racial Studies, volume 39, issue 11–12 (September–October 2016), pp. 2129–2148

Chapter 4
The discourse of racialization of labour and Chinese enterprises in Africa
Barry Sautman and Yan Hairong
Ethnic and Racial Studies, volume 39, issue 11–12 (September–October 2016), pp. 2149–2168

Chapter 5
Socioeconomic attainment, cultural tastes, and ethnic identity: class subjectivities among Uyghurs in Ürümchi
Xiaowei Zang
Ethnic and Racial Studies, volume 39, issue 11–12 (September–October 2016), pp. 2169–2186

Chapter 6
Blurring boundaries and negotiating subjectivities – the Uyghurized Han of southern Xinjiang, China
Agnieszka Joniak-Lüthi
Ethnic and Racial Studies, volume 39, issue 11–12 (September–October 2016), pp. 2187–2204

For any permission-related enquiries please visit:
http://www.tandfonline.com/page/help/permissions

Notes on Contributors

Aziz Burkhanov is an Assistant Professor at the Graduate School of Public Policy, Nazarbayev University, Astana, Kazakhstan.

Yu-Wen Chen is based at the Department of World Cultures, University of Helsinki, Helsinki, Finland.

Michael Dillon is an independent China scholar specialising in the history, politics, and society of China. He was the founding Director of the Centre for Contemporary Chinese Studies at the University of Durham, UK; is a Fellow of the Royal Historical Society and the Royal Asiatic Society; and is a member of the Royal Institute of International Affairs (Chatham House).

Ke Fan is a Professor at the Institute of Social and Cultural Anthropology, Nanjing University, Nanjing, People's Republic of China.

Agnieszka Joniak-Lüthi is 'Crossroads Asia' Research Fellow at the Department of Social and Cultural Anthropology, LMU Munich, Munich, Germany.

Hailong Ma is based at the Department of Anthropology, Sun Yat-sen University, Guangzhou, People's Republic of China.

Chow Bing Ngeow is Deputy Director of the Institute of China Studies, University of Malaya, Kuala Lumpur, Malaysia.

Barry Sautman is Visiting Professor at the Division of Social Science, Hong Kong University of Science and Technology, Kowloon, Hong Kong.

Yan Hairong is an Anthropologist in the Department of Applied Social Science, Hong Kong Polytechnic University, Kowloon, Hong Kong.

Xiaowei Zang is Chair Professor in Social Sciences at the Department of Applied Social Sciences, City University of Hong Kong, Hong Kong.

Majorities and minorities in China: an introduction

Michael Dillon

Independent Scholar, Nottinghamshire, UK

ABSTRACT
The myth of a uniformly 'Chinese' population of China must be addressed by the study of ethnic minorities, but also by questioning the nature of the Han majority, also frequently presumed to be homogeneous. Religious cultural and linguistic differences are among the most significant determinants and the parallel case of Taiwan, not under the control of the Chinese Communist Party, is also important.

Any account of China, whether in the past or today, that is not woven from threads that represent the stories of the minority ethnic groups (Mongols, Manchus, Tibetans, Uyghurs, Koreans, Miao, Yao and many others) as well as those of the Han Chinese, will be incomplete and misleading. In the West the popular stereotype is that China is a single monoculture, populated entirely by a homogeneous Chinese population who all speak the same Chinese language and have a more or less uniform Chinese culture. At its most simplistic, during the 1950s and 1960s when the country was isolated and very little reliable first-hand information was available, this was reflected in the idea of China as a 'nation of blue ants'. This notion was unwittingly strengthened by official images of the 'broad masses of the people', all seemingly clad in blue denim and marching under Maoist banners, that were published widely during the Great Leap Forward and the Cultural Revolution.

The myth of uniformity is further reinforced by the insistence of the Chinese Communist Party (CCP) and the government of the People's Republic of China (PRC) that 94 per cent of the total population can be classified as Han and that the fifty-five ethnic minorities, often referred to in the official terminology, as 'national minorities' but more accurately 'minority nationalities' [*shaoshu minzu*] only constitute 6 per cent. The way that this is often

1

presented implies that the minorities are insignificant in the overall population of China. While the official percentages may be technically correct in terms of the current official classification, they are seriously misleading, especially when the geographical distribution of ethnically diverse populations in sensitive border regions is taken into account. The way in which minorities are perceived may be changing: an authoritative report on reforms to the administration of minority regions published at the end of 2014 conceded that, 'ethnic autonomous areas account for 64 percent of the country's total land territory'.[1] This is a far more realistic appreciation of the significance of the non-Han population. Modern China cannot be understood without a clear recognition of its ethnic complexity and the impact of this complexity on social and political change and international relations.

Since China has a population of 1.3 billion and a land area the size of Europe it is hardly surprising that its demographic composition is more complex, and more interesting, than the official position allows. India is of a comparable size and is almost universally referred to as a sub-continent – although this perspective is to some extent based on the India of pre-independence days and normally includes the present-day states of Pakistan, Bangladesh and Sri Lanka. Even so there is clear recognition within India of the great variety of languages, cultures and religions in the majority Indian population alone, in addition to the scheduled castes and tribes (often referred to colloquially as 'tribals') which are in some ways comparable with the national minorities of China.[2]

Taiwan is a parallel but special case and although it does not feature in any papers in this issue it is included here in the interests of completeness. Culturally Taiwan is part of China but, as an island on the maritime frontier of southern China, it has a distinctive history and this is reflected in its ethnic composition. It was known as *Ilha Formosa* (beautiful island) to Portuguese traders and to the Dutch East India Company which established a commercial base on the island in the seventeenth century. It did not become a full province of the Chinese empire under the Manchu Qing dynasty until 1885 (two years later even than Xinjiang) when Taipei (Taibei in the *Hanyu pinyin* romanization) in the more developed north of the island was designated the provincial capital. From 1895, following the defeat of the Qing government in the first Sino-Japanese War, Taiwan became a colony of Japan. The Japanese remained the colonial masters until 1945 when Japan surrendered unconditionally at the end of the Second World War and was obliged to relinquish its overseas possessions. The influence of the colonial culture can still be seen in the architecture, the food, the spoken and written language of Taiwan and in some social and political attitudes. Since 1949 Taiwan has been *de facto* independent and has been ruled, mainly by the Kuomintang (Guomindang) Nationalist Party, as a continuation of their Republic of China administration that came to an end on the mainland after the military victory of the

Communist Party at the end of the 1946–9 civil war. Although the Nationalist government had the support of the United States during the Cold War, when Taiwan was a valuable military base close to the conflict zones of Korea and Vietnam, the *de jure* independence of the island has never been accepted by more than a small number of states, most of which have little international political influence. Since the PRC was admitted to the United Nations in October 1971 to replace the Taipei regime as the sole representative of China, many Taiwanese have complained of international isolation. Taiwan's relations with the PRC became closer in the twenty-first century but this has caused alarm among those Taiwanese who are not supporters of the Kuomintang and who fear that Chinese economic influence will eventually be extended to political domination.

Taiwan in 2013 had a population of about 23.4 million and is home to three groups of ethnic Han. The earliest settlers, who originated primarily in the province of Fujian in the southeast of the mainland, speak the Hokkien languages of that region. They migrated across the Taiwan Strait mainly in the eighteenth and nineteenth centuries. Northern Mandarin-speaking people crossed over to Taiwan with the defeated Nationalist Kuomintang in the 1940s, and there is a thriving Hakka community that has been enjoying a cultural renaissance in recent years. However, the oldest inhabitants are the distinctive indigenous ethnic groups, often referred to as 'aborigines' (*yuanzhumin*), whose languages and cultures are not remotely connected with the Han Chinese of China but are related to those of communities in Malaysia, Indonesia and the Philippines.

Han and Chinese

There is widespread confusion outside China – and to some extent within the country – between what is meant by 'Han' and 'Chinese' identities. Under the government of the PRC since 1949, and in what the Chinese Communist Party perceives as the interests of national unity, there has been an attempt to establish a single national identity – the concept of *Zhongguoren* (Chinese in the sense of citizen of China) – with which the whole population is expected to identify. The Han (or Han Chinese) are the majority population who speak one of the languages (sometimes misleadingly referred to as dialects) that are grouped together as Chinese and whose written language and culture is expressed through the medium of Chinese characters. Even this is not as straightforward as it might appear as two distinct versions of the Chinese script are in current use. Traditional full-form characters are used in Taiwan, by most people in Hong Kong and in émigré Chinese communities in Europe, Australasia and North America. Simplified characters (modified in the 1950s as part of a mainland campaign to reform the language in the interests of greater literacy) are standard on the mainland, and are increasingly used elsewhere as the global reach of the PRC has extended. Because the traditional script is used in Hong Kong where the dominant spoken language is Cantonese, the misapprehension has sometimes arisen that it is a Cantonese script. However it is also used by Mandarin speakers in Hong Kong, Taiwan and elsewhere. There are in fact additional characters used to represent Cantonese speech but they are only used in special circumstances.

The Chinese (Han) spoken languages include Mandarin (*putonghua*) – used mainly in northern China but also in the southwest – and the very different southeastern languages which include Cantonese, Fujianese (Min or Hokkien), Shanghainese (Wu) and Hakka. Because speakers of all these languages use the same Chinese script it is assumed that they are simply dialects of one Chinese language: in practice these spoken forms are mutually incomprehensible and are as different from each other as are Portuguese, Italian and Romanian (all members of the Romance family of languages) in Europe. There are also dialects or sub-dialects of all of the main variants of Chinese. However speakers of all of these languages are considered to be Han and are also likely to identify themselves as such. This is in contrast to minorities such as the Uyghurs, Mongolians, Tibetans or Miao, all of whom have their own spoken languages and, in most cases, scripts.[3]

As this complexity indicates, the concept of a single monolithic Han culture is not tenable; even within the Han family there is a complex pattern of identities. The modern Communist state and its Nationalist predecessors have sought to play down these differences in the interests of national unity. At times, particularly at the time of writing and in the light of conflict in Tibet and Xinjiang, even drawing attention to such differences can invite accusations of lending support to groups that wished to 'split' China – assumed (in the face of incontrovertible historical evidence) to have existed for several thousand years as a single unified state.[4]

To understand the problems behind these assumptions, it is necessary to examine the changing nature of majorities, minorities and the changing frontiers of China. In present-day China some regions, especially border regions, are predominantly non-Han. Outside China, Tibet is the best known of these distinctive cultures but this is assumed to be a special case and simply the result of a Chinese invasion in 1959 of a state which was previously completely independent of China. The truth is inevitably more complicated: Tibet was part of the Chinese empire under the Manchus and today there are Tibetan communities within China but outside central Tibet (the Tibetan Autonomous Region) which also overlap with other communities, especially those of the Muslim Hui. The case for Tibetan independence has been well-argued and widely publicized, and has powerful support within the exiled Tibetan community in Dharamsala and more widely. Similar demands by Mongols and Uyghurs, who live in border regions adjacent to Tibet, where they are, or once were, the majority populations and whose claims for auton-omy are as legitimate as those of the Tibetans, are less familiar in the West.

Ethnic groups in China

It is not possible in an introduction of this length to cover in detail all fifty-six ethnic groups in the PRC (the Han and fifty-five groups officially designated as minorities), many of which are small in number. Some of these minorities are discussed in the articles by the contributing authors but it is important to acknowledge the diversity of ethnic groups in China and the relationship that they have with the rest of Chinese society.

There are important differences between the way of life of ethnic minority groups in the cities and the countryside, especially in the more remote rural areas, including the grasslands of Tibet, the oases of Xinjiang and the steppes of Mongolia where minorities may in practice be the majority popu-lations. In cities and large towns minorities may well live in the same areas and be in the same employment as the Han – teaching, office work, shop assist-ants, etc. – and may also dress in a similar fashion, especially the younger gen-eration for whom a youth culture may be more important than outward signs of ethnic belonging. However, even in the cities there are certain areas where minority groups settle and these areas may well take on the flavour of tra-ditional communities in the minority homelands – for example, Hui and Uyghur areas (some of which have now been demolished) in Beijing. In the more remote rural areas minority cultures flourish with less influence from the majority Han and the distinctiveness of smaller ethnic groups in the way they dress, eat, live and behave is more evident in the countryside.

The historical dimension should not be ignored. Ethnic groups are not frozen in time: many communities, and individuals within them, have become accommodated or assimilated to a greater or lesser extent to the norms of other groups with which they have come into contact, particularly to the language and customs of the dominant Han, whether willingly or not. Accommodation is of course only one possible response to contact. In other cases it has led to resistance, a determination to assert the distinctive identity of the minority, or the development of movements to attain political independence such as those that have from time to time emerged among the Hui, the Uyghurs, the Mongols and the Tibetans.

Religious, cultural and linguistic differences

Religious differences are an important marker of the division between ethnic groups. Most Tibetans and Mongolians are Buddhists but their traditions, sacred texts and the language of worship are not the same as those of Chinese Buddhists. Hui and Uyghur communities are Muslim by tradition and mostly by belief, and in both groups their religion is an integral part of their identity; however they do not pray in the same mosques or eat in the same halal restaurants and they are treated quite differently by the PRC government. There are Christian religious minorities among the Han as well as among minority groups and these religious differences overlap with ethnic differences. Followers of new religions, especially Falungong, are sometimes treated as members of an oppressed minority – the activities of Falungong have indeed been ruthlessly suppressed by the government of the PRC – but there is no real similarity with the position of ethnic minorities. Many, probably the great majority of, adherents of Falungong are from the majority Han community.[5]

Most ethnic minorities in China have their own languages which distinguish them from the Han but also from other minorities. The differences between the languages of the minorities may be quite significant but in some cases, especially where small populations are involved, they are less so to the linguistic analyst, although it is usually important to the different groups that they preserve these distinctions, however slight. It is a policy of the PRC government that *putonghua* (Standard Chinese or Mandarin) should be taught in schools in ethnic minority regions as well as in Han communities. The spoken form is a standardized version of northern Mandarin, based the pronunciation of Beijing. It was the national language (*guoyu*) of China under the Guomindang Nationalists (and still is on Taiwan) and is the continuation of *guanhua* (official language), the lingua franca of the Chinese empire under the Manchu Qing dynasty. There is resistance to this policy in minority areas and even among some Han communities such as Cantonese speakers in the south. Some minority organizations, notably those claiming to represent Tibetans and Uyghurs, consider that even a bilingual language teaching environment would inevitably favour *putonghua* and is therefore a real or potential threat to the indigenous non-Chinese languages. The level of competence in Standard Chinese among ethnic minorities ranges from the truly bilingual to virtually none, depending on the ability and outlook of the individuals and the attitudes of the community in which they live: a similar range of abilities is found among the less educated Han speakers of southern Chinese languages.

Major differences from the Han are also apparent in minority social practices, particularly those that relate to courtship, marriage, birth and death, although some of these have been lost as China has modernized under a Han-dominated Communist Party. The CCP has been determined to abolish practices identified as superstitious, feudal and backward, although its success in this has been mixed. Traditional music, dance and theatre have usually survived, encouraged to some extent by the government as acceptable expressions of ethnic minority culture that do not threaten the political status quo. To what extent the presentation of minority cultures in contemporary China is a genuine representation of a living culture rather than a sanitized version to satisfy official claims of 'the great unity of the nationalities' [*minzu da tuanjie*] is much disputed and varies from case to case.

Han majority

Although this special issue of *Ethnic and Racial Studies* is devoted to the non-Han population of China, the Han majority cannot be ignored. In China the Han are typically viewed, explicitly or implicitly, as the most advanced of the ethnic groups and they are the standard against which minorities are measured, however inappropriate that might seem to members of minority groups or independent thinkers.

The origins of the use of the word 'Han' to denote an ethnic group are in *Hanren* (people of Han) that was used to refer to the subjects of the Han dynasty (206 BC–220 AD), widely regarded as the period which first saw the flowering of traditional Chinese culture, and their descendants. By the sixth century AD, Han had come to mean the settled agricultural communities of the Central Plains as distinct from the nomadic pastoralists of the northern and western frontiers or the tribes to the south who were considered to be less civilized. Another term, *Tangren* (people of Tang) was used in a similar way after the Tang dynasty (618–907), the second great flowering of Chinese culture but one that incorporated many elements of Central and Inner Asian cultures; this term was mainly applied to the Han Chinese of the south and this can be seen in contemporary Chinatowns in Britain and the rest of Europe which are often called *Tangrenjie* (Streets of the Tang People), reflecting the origins of most of the communities in migrants from Guangdong and other southern provinces. In Singapore and the Chinese diaspora in other parts of Asia, the term 'Hua', a word for Chinese which also means 'glorious' or 'flowery' is preferred to 'Han' and this is preserved in the mainland term for overseas Chinese, *huaqiao*.

The Qing dynasty (1644–1911) was founded and was ruled by Manchus but increasingly relied on Han Chinese officials for its government. As it drew to a close, towards the end of the nineteenth century Chinese radicals, blaming the Manchus for the serious internal and external problems that the nation faced, began to emphasize the need for the Han to rise up against their alien rulers. An influential book, *Qiushu* (Book of Compulsion), written by Zhang Binglin in 1900, is an important example of the way in which the cultural and linguistic closeness of the Han people, and their difference from the ruling Manchus and their Mongol allies, was expressed as a racial unity with a common blood lineage that could be traced back to the mythical Yellow Emperor, who by tradition ruled around 2500 BC.[6] When the Qing dynasty finally collapsed in 1911, the Republican administration that succeeded it rejected this analysis and in its place emphasized the role of the Han as the most advanced group in a mixed society: the PRC has effectively followed in this tradition, although discussions of the ethnic minorities and the Han are couched in Marxist terminology that owes much to the model of the Soviet Union under Stalin.

Since 94 per cent of the population of China are classified as Han, and according to the census of 2000 there were approximately 1.1 billion of them, this would qualify them as the largest ethnic group in the world if they could be considered as one single homogeneous group. Given the geographical spread of Han communities from the far northeast in what was once called Manchuria to the borders of Burma and Vietnam, from conservative Beijing southwards to livelier and more cosmopolitan and commercially minded cities such as Shanghai in the east of China and Guangzhou close to the border with Hong Kong, it would be surprising if all Han could be classified as a single culturally identical ethnic group. Although on one level Han people are comfortable with identifying themselves as part of this majority group, on another there is also a large measure of agreement on differences between the Han of one area and another. Beijingers, Shanghainese and Cantonese all have stereotypical views of each other – southerners frequently characterize Beijingers as stuffy and pompous (in the same way that other Scandinavians stereotype Stockholmers). There are recognized subgroups of Han, some of which suffer discrimination, one of the best documented being the Subei people of northern Jiangsu who are the butt of jokes similar to those directed at the Kerrymen in Ireland. The Han can be subdivided most easily according to the languages that they speak but also, especially in the rural areas, by different local customs in such matters as marriage, childrearing and religious worship. In spite of the fact that Han people are far from being homogeneous, minorities are often defined in terms of how they differ from the generalized Han.

The articles in this special China issue of *Ethnic and Racial Studies* present new, and sometimes unusual, perspectives on ethnic relations in China and interactions between China and other cultures. Two major themes run through this set of papers: the classification of ethnic minorities in China by the state and its implications; and the way in which China and the Chinese are seen by outsiders as well as insiders. The contributors are from a wide range of backgrounds and are currently based in China, Hong Kong, Malaysia, Kazakhstan and Germany. The subjects of their research are the politics of minority classification in the PRC; questions of identity in Xinjiang; Kazakhstani perceptions of China and the Chinese; Chinese Muslims in Malaysia; and the growing Chinese diaspora in Africa.

In his 'Representation of Ethnic Minorities in Socialist China', Fan Ke from the Institute of Social and Cultural Anthropology at Nanjing University examines the way that ethnicity has been represented in the PRC since 1949. The ethnic configuration of fifty-six 'nationalities', which is based on a re-categorization of the entire population, has broadly speaking been accepted by most of the population of China. Even if they do not agree with parts of this classification, which some members of minority groups do not, it is the one that is commonly used. The origins of this system are complex but arise primarily from a group of projects that were launched as part of the CCP's programme of 'state-making and nation-building' in the 1950s, in particular one that was begun in 1956 and focused on the investigation of the social history of ethnic minorities. Fan Ke examines the way in which the official forms of narration and representation of ethnic minorities emerged and how the representation of ethnic minorities functions in the construction of the Chinese nation. The official classification of ethnic minorities in China that was used with little modification between 1949 and the 1980s was not based on an objective or scientific analysis of cultural differences. The system of classification that emerged 'was produced through a top-down process' that was intended primarily to serve the interests of the party-state. It emphasized common features rather than differences and was an integral part of the project to construct a new version of 'Zhonghua Minzu, the Chinese nation' after the establishment of the PRC in 1949.

'More Islamic, No Less Chinese: Explorations into Overseas Chinese Muslim Identities in Malaysia' by Peter Ngeow Chow Bing of the Institute of China Studies at the University of Malaya, is a valuable reminder of the transnational implications of ethnic differences in the Chinese world. The article focuses on Muslims in the Chinese diaspora in Malaysia. These Chinese Muslims are a relatively new component of the wider Chinese community in Malaysia. They are Muslims from China (predominantly Chinese-speaking Hui rather than Uyghurs or other Xinjiang people), most of whom arrived in Malaysia as students in the late 1980s. As such they are part of the Overseas Chinese diaspora which has a long and distinguished history in Malaysia but, as Muslims, they have a different relationship to the majority Malay population, which is predominantly Muslim. Ngeow Chow Bing raises the question of whether this 'connection with and exposure to the wider Islamic world will reinforce or challenge their identity as Chinese Muslims'. The paper is based on a study of the activities of the Overseas Chinese Muslim Association, interviews with members of the Chinese Muslim elite and data from a survey of Chinese Muslim students in Malaysia. Chinese Muslims in Malaysia appear to be comfortable with their joint identity as both Muslim and Chinese and are able to utilize this status to enhance their economic and social position. While Islam is clearly of central importance to members of this community, they do not reject their Chinese heritage and this aspect of their dual identity is reinforced by the presence in Malaysia of a sizable ethnic Chinese minority, who are not Muslims.

In 'Kazakh Perspectives on China, the Chinese and Chinese Migration', Aziz Burkhanov and Yu-Wen Chen from Nazarbayev University in Kazakhstan demonstrate that the views of Kazakhstanis on China and the Chinese are both complex and divided. Using a discourse analysis of articles from newspapers in the different languages of Kazakhstan they demonstrate that the official discourse in state-sponsored Russian- and Kazakh-language newspapers is broadly in agreement with the country's policy of developing its engagement with its expanding Chinese neighbour. In contrast, in independent Kazakh-language newspapers it is common to come across negative stereotypes of China and the Chinese, as well as more extreme attitudes which can be categorized as Sinophobia. Independent Russian-language newspapers have a more sophisticated attitude towards China, but most exhibit a veiled inclination to be critical of the country and its people. Although the majority of these organs of mass communication have no direct impact on Kazakhstan's policies towards China, they are an important indicator of social views in Kazakhstan that have to be taken into account by the country's ruling elite which has to balance its relations with China against securing 'the stability and legitimacy of the regime'.

'The discourse of racialization of labour and Chinese enterprises in Africa' by Barry Sautmann and Yan Hairong of the Hong Kong University of Science and Technology looks even further afield to the interaction between African employees and Chinese employers as the expanding Chinese economy began to have a significant impact on the African continent. Their research shows that 'racialized ideas of difference and hierarchy do affect Chinese enterprises in Africa' but that this is not primarily the result of Chinese attitudes towards Africans as often suggested in some influential Western writing on the subject. Contrary to some widely publicized analyses, neither is the racialization of the relationship between management and employees the sole responsibility of the employer. Rather it arises from actions by Chinese employers, African employees and Western actors. The rhetoric of 'racialization of African employees by some Chinese employers and African employee and politicians' racialization of Chinese, show that South–South racializations of labour markedly differ from the North–South exemplar'. The authors find that, although the racialization of labour does exist in the relationship between Chinese and Africans, it is not possible to conclude whether growing contact between the two cultures will exacerbate or ease the problem.

Two papers, researched and written independently, reveal the complexity of identification and self-identification in the Xinjiang Uyghur Autonomous Region. Based on data drawn from a survey conducted in Ürümchi in 2007, Xiaowei Zang, in 'Socioeconomic attainment, cultural tastes, and ethnic identity: class subjectivities among Uyghurs in Ürümchi', examines Uyghurs' subjective perception of their class status in Ürümchi, the capital city of Xinjiang, and shows that income and occupational attainment are not closely correlated with Uyghur choices of class labels. Uyghur ethnic identity also has an impact on how Ürümchi Uyghurs make choices of class labels. They consider themselves to be a subordinate group and generally compare themselves unfavourably with Han Chinese when identifying their perceived level of social class. The effect of this is that intergroup competition between Uyghurs and the Han eclipses the variations in socioeconomic attainments among the different Uyghur groups. The implication of these results for other minority groups in China is also discussed.

In 'Blurring boundaries and negotiating subjectivities – the Uyghurized Han of southern Xinjiang, China', Agnieszka Joniak-Lüthi explores one process of negotiating collective subjectivities among the 'Uyghurized Han' living in the southern part of the Xinjiang Uyghur Autonomous Region, a predominantly Uyghur region in which the Han constitute less than a quarter of the population. The paper is based on research material collected as part of a long-term project of ethnographic fieldwork. The author argues that 'Uyghurized Han creatively construct a sense of belonging in Xinjiang by positioning themselves at the interface of Han-ness and Uyghur-ness'. This is achieved through a process of 'contradictory but nonetheless simultaneous processes of blurring and fixing boundaries of identity' in their relationship with both the Han and other Uyghurs. It is this process of boundary negotiation which produces collective subjectivities.

This paper also addresses issues relating to the classification of ethnic identity (*minzu*) that were also raised in the article by Fan Ke. When the project to classify *minzu* was initiated in the 1950s, research teams were deployed to multiethnic areas to identify the *minzu* and classify them with respect to their level of 'historical, cultural, social, and material advancement'. The assumption was that these categories were firmly established and, as such, were a reliable guide for the organs of state administering the minority areas. Although official designations are unalterable without complicated political and administrative procedures, a complicated web of subjective identities has evolved which supplements, and potentially undermines, the official categories. Academic researchers, both Chinese and overseas, and activists working on behalf of some ethnic groups, are frequently critical of the official designations which are at odds with the self-identification of some groups. Although there have been a number of proposals for re-classification and for the inclusion of new categories, such as Chinese Jews, there is no evidence at the time of writing that the Chinese government is minded to respond positively to this criticism.

Notes

1. 'China to favor minority officials in ethnically-diverse regions', *Xinhua News Agency*, 22 December 2014.

2. These comparative observations were informed by discussions with staff and students at Jawaharlal Nehru University, New Delhi in 2012. See also Sunil Janah *The Tribals of India* Delhi: Oxford University Press, 1993.

3. Thurgood, Graham and Randy J. Lapolla (eds.) *The Sino-Tibetan Languages* Abingdon: Routledge, 2003 provides up to date and authoritative information on Chinese languages and dialects in addition to related languages outside China.

4. This issue is exemplified by the case of Ilham Tohti, an economist of Uyghur origin who had been teaching at the prestigious Nationalities University (*Minzu Daxue*) in Beijing. In September 2014 he was sentenced to life imprisonment and the confiscation of his property (including his life savings) for having allowed discussion of the Xinjiang issue on a website and at the university, *Radio Free Asia* 24 September 2014.

5. Michael Dillon *Religious Minorities in China* London: Minority Rights Group, 2001.

6. Zhang Binglin (selected and edited by Xiang Shiling) *Qiushu* Shenyang: Liaoning People's Press, 1994.

Representation of ethnic minorities in socialist China

Ke Fan

Institute of Social and Cultural Anthropology, Nanjing University, Nanjing, People's Republic of China

ABSTRACT

This study examines the fact of representation of ethnicity in the People's Republic of China. The present ethnic configuration, centred on a re-categorization of the population, came to be accepted by ordinary people in Chinese society as the result of the multiple projects in association with state-making and nation-building. This paper delineates how the projects in question came about, especially the one focused on the investigation of ethnic minority social history. It examines the way in which narrating and representing ethnic minorities officially took place and how the representation of ethnic minorities functions in the construction of the Chinese nation. It argues that representation for ethnicities focused on how to locate each of them at a certain stage of social development, conceptualizing the Chinese nation in a framework of brotherhood in order to include those excluded by the mainstream throughout history.

Introduction

This paper examines the representation of ethnicity in the People's Republic of China (hereinafter PRC). How has this representation come about, in what ways has the representation supplied the engineering of the search for national solidarity in which the party-state has engaged ever since, and how and why have some forms of this representation changed in recent decades? Before going further, the term representation should be defined. Representation in this article is not what is usually thought of, that is as an institutionally based categorization of the population in contemporary China. Instead, it refers to one that is produced to provide service to politics out of this categorization. It is all about how peoples of ethnic minorities are culturally or socially presented or represented through manipulation by the party-state. Representation, in this sense is more likely to be as Stuart

Hall defined it. According to Hall, representation could be all forms of languages. According to Hall, 'languages work through representation', that is 'not because they are all written or spoken (they are not), but because they are all use some element to stand for or represent what we want to say, to express or to communicate a thought, concept, idea or feeling'(2003, 4). For Hall, there are all kinds of language, such as spoken, written, music, and even fashion. However, unlike Hall, in this study, representation is not about what people in question want to say but what the party-state attempts to say as spokesperson for the people who are represented.

In a socialist state, a body of systematic knowledge about ethnic minorities is produced under the state's guidance. All things regarding ethnic minorities are strictly written, composed, made, and produced in the same framework or by the same elements, eventually expressing what the state wants to say. This is the reason this article treats it as representation and its production as top-down: the state initiated this process. In recent decades, ethnic minority people have more often than not actively produced representations for themselves, in which cultural elements are particularly addressed. Changes in this way could be considered to be bottom-up. Nonetheless, this is not what concerns this article.

Scholars have carried out significant research on the question of how ethnic minorities are culturally represented in China. It has been argued that, in addition to backwardness in social and economic developments, they are frequently romantically portrayed as talented in dancing and singing (*nengge shanwu*); some of them are also depicted as having some degree of free sexual life before or even after marriage (Harrell 1995; Gladney 1994; Tapp 2002; Yu 2000). They were more often than not feminized in the cultural representations that mainstream society has produced even long before the initial ethnic classification (Gladney 1994; Tapp 2002; Yu 2000).

The formation of imagination as such should be attributed to a long time discourse that has been diffused through the modern education system, media, films, and other cultural productions. This discourse has served the state so has to be congruent with the state's political agenda. As a consequence, the state eventually represents ethnic minorities' heritage, 'socializes them into a national identity, structures their education opportunities and links their schooling to economic development' (Postiglione 1999; Zhao and Postiglione 2010). Accordingly, ethnic representation from 1949 onward has varied in response to the changing content of national identity anxiety (Chen 2008). Therefore, what the observer obtains from the representation in question is less about ethnic minorities per se and more about 'the presence of certain state ideological messages' (Yu 2000).

There seems no objection to the view that representation about ethnic minorities after the establishment of the People's Republic has been constructed in a direction that the state determines. This does not deny the fact that the representation in question has varied with changing circumstances. Accordingly, whether it is in museums (Fiskesjö 2015; Varutti 2011; Vickers 2007), theme parks (Anagnost 1997; Gladney 1994; Tapp 2002), the media, schools (Anagnost 1997; Postiglione 1999; Zhao and Postiglione 2010), or in other cultural productions (Anagnost 1997; Chen 2008; Harrell 1995; Yu 2000), what has been presented is consistent with what the state has needed at certain period of time.

There have been many descriptions of ethnic minorities throughout Chinese history. These descriptions have produced some stereotypes about ethnic minorities, which, in turn, have also appeared in the representation in question. But descriptions in the past are different from the representations that we see today for at least three reasons: First, even though the state today uses the same designations for a number of the ethnic minorities, these past references to various ethnic groups were not rationally and systematically determined as 'bound seriality' (Anderson 1998, 29; also see Chatterjee 2004, 5–6). In recent years, however, some of messages from the remote past have been 'rediscovered' for commercial reasons (see Fan 2015, 23–31; Fiskesjö 2015). Second, the diffusion of these classifiers before the formation of the PRC was very limited. Third, the names of the ethnic groups in the past were not systematically produced under state supervision as they were in modern times.

Almost all studies mentioned above have focused on how ethnic minorities are presented in terms of cultural matters. However, they have barely examined the process of how cultural representation of ethnic minorities as a political task took shape in the 1950s. This study attempts to fill that gap.

Comparing ethnic representations produced before and after the establishment of PRC reveals how the state demarcated boundaries for ethnic minorities. My point is that the present ethnic configuration centreing on a re-categorization of the population came to be accepted by ordinary people as a result of a long process in which multiple projects in association with state-making and nation-building, respectively, took place. Having taken an approach of historical anthropology, as a qualitative study this analysis first describes how the projects in question came about, especially the investigation of ethnic minority social history. Next, it examines ways in which narrating and representing ethnic minorities officially took place and how the representation in question functions in the construction of the Chinese nation (zhonghua minzu).

The projects and the 'scientific knowledge' production about ethnic minorities

Ethnic identification was the most important work the Chinese party-state engaged in during the decades since 1953. From the very beginning, it was a component part of state-making engineering that aimed to establish People's Congress system (Fan 2012). This campaign, which was officially announced as complete in 1987, resulted in the identification of 55 minority nationalities (shaoshu minzu). This classification project fitted the state's modernity campaign well. Thus, the party-state attempted to fully control the areas where ethnic minorities had lived throughout history and where there were frontiers with other states. In addition, the project was an activity showing that the Chinese Communist Party (hereinafter the CCP) had kept its promises made to ethnic minorities when these minorities aided the revolutionary struggle. Only after establishing how many ethnic minorities lived in China could the party-state carry out its preferential policy toward national minorities and pursue its policy of allowing ethnic representation in the institutions of power (see Fan 2012), for instance, every separate minority nationality would have rights of having their representatives sit in People's Representative Congresses and of having positions in governmental apparatuses as well. More importantly, a separate minority nationality could establish its autonomous ethnic regions, ranking from county to provincial levels, if their population size was more than 22 per cent of a total population of the region. Having helped to establish political representation for ethnic minority, this project led to the other project coming about. It, in turn, initiated the production of representation of ethnic minorities that is the focus of this article.

The investigation into the social history of minority nationalities was trigged in 1956. It aimed to collect data among ethnic minorities in order to search for ways to legitimize the categorization of ethnic minorities, which was still ongoing under the ethnic identification project. The new project also helped identify minority nationalities since the data allowed policy makers to incorporate some ethnic groups into separate minority nationalities according to their historical connections and cultural similarities (see Huang and Shi 2005, 125). The other important purpose of this social history project was to 'save (qiangjiu) social, historical, and cultural heritages' (Chen 1999; Ma 1999).

This investigation collected a wealth of materials from ethnic minorities nationwide. From 1956 to 1958, some twenty minority nationalities, including Mongols, Tibetans, Uyghurs, and Zhuang, among many others, were investigated. Starting from 1958, the investigation teams were increased from eight to sixteen. They undertook investigations in sixteen provinces and ethnic autonomous districts. As a result more than 314 items regarding the history and social conditions of different ethnic minorities were produced; more than 100 items of archives and other documents collected; and, more than 10 documentary films made. Drawing on these materials, fifty-seven items of different kinds, ranging from concise histories to historiographies of most separate minority nationalities, were published. Accordingly, the state announced to the public, after 'completion' of the social history project in late 1964, that, 'for the first time, the government had got [sic] to know the basic situations of minority nationalities in terms of their origins, economic and sociopolitical structures, ideologies, customs and habits, and religious beliefs and practices' (Huang and Shi 2005, 162). Not only did this project serve the project of ethnic identification in terms of regrouping ethnic minorities but it also resulted in a body of systemic knowledge regarding what ethnic minorities produced. The social history project, therefore, also functioned as a means of categorizing the population.

The social history investigation and its works disembedded the social relations of ethnic minorities from their local context; the spatial and temporal existence of ethnic minorities has been greatly reorganized (to paraphrase the discussion of modernity by Giddens (1990, 21)). Even though the cultural representations that powered this reorganization essentially served a Real-Politik, it did nevertheless impel people to ponder their own subjectivity and group memberships. Therefore, the production of rational knowledge (Giddens 1990), or the 'scientification' of knowledge (Elias 1998, 217–245) was not only a task for state officials and scholars but also a process joined in by the peoples subjected to the state's social policy in their cultural inventions and performances.

What concerns this study is to what extent or in what ways has the state, through those campaigns and projects, provided a blueprint that has brought about the production of ethnic representation. Drawing upon certain kinds of the evolutionary imagination, this blueprint was schematized. The investigation in question thus brought a completely different narrative about the ethnic minorities of China. This narrative was, however, according to the leadership of the party-state, also a contribution to so-called 'scientific' knowledge about human beings. I am not questioning the reliability of the facts this narrative might have provided but questioning how those facts were generalized.

Representing national minorities

The year 1959 was important in the history of the PRC. With the 'Great Leap Forward' (*dayuejin*) in the sector of economic construction, the central government led the country into the completion of the system of a centrally planned economy. As long as the market was no longer a central concern in economic operation, the government needed only to employ political propaganda and slogans to create zeal for advancing the economy. One could only understand this operation in terms of governmentality, that is, the goal of making the governed believe their will could be realized under the governance, paraphrasing from Foucault (2000, 201–222). It is therefore not difficult to understand why China should have had a slogan such as 'Catch up economically with Britain in fifteen years' in its economic construction.

This combination of economic construction and ideological movement was implemented by the state to enhance its legitimacy during an era when its authority was not yet really established. What happened in 1959 was an example of action the state undertook in order to fix its authority and legitimacy in the heart of its citizens. The year of 1959 symbolizes that the new state had completed its first ten-year term, which was considered long enough to assess its achievements. The Chinese take these ten-year anniversaries quite seriously. Every decade the Chinese call for an especially large celebration (daqing) for the National Days. The decade is thus significant in Chinese politics, especially in terms of searching for national identity, since opportunities for the practice of the 'civil religion' which supports the state are provided at these times.

For the tenth anniversary of the establishment of PRC, the entire country was mobilized to contribute to an atmosphere of celebration under state guidance. Every place in China was required to offer presents (xianli) for the anniversary. Accordingly, the year 1959 became a meaningful conjuncture for the display of the PRC's achievements in all areas. The ten grand buildings, represented by the Great Hall of the People's Congress (renmin dahuitang), were completed not only as an architectural representation of the prosperity of the socialist motherland but also as primary symbols of the reconstruction of the nation and of the superior power of the state. As one of these ten grand architectures, the Cultural Palace of Nationalities (CPN, minzu wenhuagong) was particularly designed as a showcase through which the state could present its accomplishments in the area of minority works (minzu gongzuo) by demonstrating how the state takes care of minority nationalities.

The framework for the official narrative of minority nationalities was also set up at this time. A central government document located in the Fujian Provincial Archive (FPA 128-2-980, 1) demonstrates that it was for the purpose of celebrating National Day in 1959, that the state first began to be officially engaged in the project of writing national history. This seemed to be a consequence of the social history project. Not only did the state allocate tasks of this writing to different areas nationwide under the charge of different levels of government but it also drafted outlines to every component part of this project.

Though there have been discussions on the relationship between ethnic minorities and the majority Han since Chinese nationalism emerged in the late nineteenth century, 1959 was the first time that ethnic minorities were officially drawn in to be included in the construction of the Chinese nation (zhonghua minzu). But, the problem is that as long as one employs key words such as development, evolution, and progress to measure peoples, sorting them out according to different stages of their social development, the cultural value and dignity of these people must inevitably be somewhat downplayed or twisted. People such as Jingpo (Kachin, as in Burma) were described as primitive, on the bottom level of social development implying that they would need help from those who are advanced. They have, ever since, been mostly stigmatized as backward in all aspects of their existence. This case demonstrates that the generality of the grand narrative drawn up for these people therefore faces inherent challenges because soon or later people such as Jingpo would begin to feel insulted.

According to a notice issued by the State Council (FPA 128-2-980, 1), in order to get ready for the completion of the CPN before 1 May 1959, officials in all provinces and autonomous districts with minority nationalities were asked to collect materials, books, archives, and any other things that could reflect the minorities' progress and historical change. It was said in this notice that a museum and a library would be the two most important components of the 'palace'. The tasks of these components would be:

> propagating the great victory of the Party's policy towards minority nationalities and its brilliant achievements of works with minority nationalities in the past ten years; reflecting accomplishments the minority nationalities have achieved under the leadership of the CCP in all aspects of politics, economics, and culture …; and introducing our country's minority peoples' excellent tradition of bravery and industriousness and great intelligence, as well as their contributions to the motherland's history, culture, revolutionary struggle and to the cause of socialist construction. (FPA 128-2-980, 1)

These examples evidence how political power was engaged in both the production of knowledge and cultivation of its citizens.

Both the museum and the library would function for the purpose of propaganda. According to the State Council, the purpose of both the museum and library in the CPN was to:

> provide the referential materials relating to studies concerning national questions to the broad masses of the people, professionals within ethnic minorities nationwide, and relevant bodies; And, through display and exhibition as well as through books, [we] would provide education in both patriotism and internationalism to people of every national minority, and therefore arouse their enthusiasm to participate in the construction of the great-socialist motherland big family. (FPA 128-2-980, 1)

For this purpose all cultural and historical relics and documentary materials that were going to be displayed had to be carefully selected. A draft outline for the comprehensive exhibition in the CPN museum provided a chart showing how an officially cultural representation of ethnic minorities worked out. It was actually not just a guide for organizing the exhibition but also a schema for writing a grand narrative for the newly established nation-state. The objective of the comprehensive exhibition was declared to be as follows.

[It would] summarily reflect both the fundamental policies and great achievements of the Party and state in terms of national work, and indicate that our country has become a unified multinational state in the beginning through specific examples. All peoples of national minorities are brave and industrious, having made great contributions to founding the motherland and supporting the cause of socialist construction. With the development of the socialist revolution and cause of socialist construction, especially since the Great Leap Forward, a new socialist interethnic relationship of socialism has formed and developed. (FPA 128-2-980, 11)

Thus, the outline emphasized that each display should have captions and should present national policy through exhibiting the documents or, at least the policy written in abstracts but, more importantly, should display pictures, objects, relics, scale models, and replicas of minority life and customs. By doing so, the exhibition would 'specifically and in a lively manner manifest the spirit of interethnic equality, unity, brotherhood, and cooperation, reflecting a prosperous new atmosphere of development of nationalities' (FPA 128-2-980, 11).

The above simple manifesto was followed by very detailed contents characterizing this 'display outline' (chenlie dagang). The display was designed to have ten parts as shown in Table 1. Each part encompasses several sub-parts according to different topics and issues (FPA 128-2-980, 11–29). All of those took shape in a framework emphasizing the development and progress that the CCP had brought to minority nationalities. The outlines were so specific, even asking for particular pictures for the display according to the different topics. All the captions were of course basically clichés that in themselves may not warrant serious attention. They are nevertheless a living example of how 'ideological knowledge' came into existence (Elias 1994, 109).

To be sure, this ideal and abstract schema was based upon the data collected from the investigation, which was still going on. As two other documents attached to the display outline indicate, some specific topics were extremely lacking in data. Some phrases even reflected a conscious

Table 1. Display outline for the 1959 comprehensive exhibition in the CPN.

1. Prologue
2. Our country has been an unified multi-national state since its early beginnings
3. The establishment of the PRC: the beginning of a new era with interethnic equality and freedom
4. The carrying out of the system of autonomous districts for nationalities and protecting the right to interethnic equality for those who are living scattered among other peoples
5. Establishment of the Party and Communist Youth League and cultivation of cadres among minorities
6. The party undertaking work of united front (tongyi zhanxian) among persons who are in the upper class of minorities
7. The policy of freedom in religious beliefs
8. Democratic reform and socialist transformation
9. Economic construction
10. Cultural construction

awareness that certain difficulties were hard to overcome because the outline provided was so uniform for all provinces and ethnic autonomous districts. Thus, on 5 April 1959, the Office for the Celebration of National Day in the CPN put forward some questions for discussion and distributed them nationwide (FPA 128-2-980, 6). The form of these questions (see Table 2) acknowledges that a uniform approach to narrating historiography for ethnic minorities would have to leave out regional or even ethnic diversities and specific historical processes in different regions and localities.

These questions reveal that the exhibition illustrating the success of the CCP's policy towards national minorities was fundamentally a political task to be carried out not only in Beijing but also nationwide.

Another document issued by the State Cultural Ministry and State Commission for Nationality Affairs on 9 June 1959 (FPA 128-2-980, 4–5) called for the provision of more ethnic artifacts (minzu wenwu). From this official document, one can clearly perceive why such a general overarching narrative would necessarily have to be partially invented or fictionalized. The notice said:

> The Chinese Revolutionary Museum, Chinese Historical Museum, and the CPN will be completed respectively during June and July. Currently, all three are tentatively displaying cultural artifacts that they have collected. According to the situation right now, because of the lack of ethnic relics, it is difficult for the displays to portray a full view of the history created by all nationalities and their revolutionary struggle. ... The above three museums therefore ask provinces (districts) to organize some relevant offices to give energetic support to the museums by providing ethnic relics as follows .... (FPA 128-2-980, 4)

What the three museums called for were materials that could manifest the interaction, mutual influence, and communication that has historically taken place between different nationalities and that could reflect how ethnic minorities had participated in the Chinese revolution since the 1840s. These materials were to consist of artifacts and documents.

From the records cited above, one can conclude that there were actually only two main themes: First, the importance of minority people's group membership in the construction of national history. Second, all great changes had taken place among those people under the leadership of CCP. These two themes have been retained and are the same even today.

Table 2. Questions for discussion on the historical part of the exhibition, 5 April 1959.

1. Should all provinces and autonomous districts have an historical part?
2. If the history must be part of exhibition is it appropriate to reflect the history of one or two minority nationalities in an area and leave the others out?
3. Does the display need to address the history of revolutionary struggle or the history of interethnic oppression or both?
4. If the history must be included when should it start?
5. What is the size or proportion of the historical part in every display?

Inclusion of the excluded through a constructed hierarchical brotherhood

In socialist China, until the middle 1980s cultural particularities of ethnic minorities were not a real concern in the domain of cultural production. What is important for the party-state is to include those minorities who have been excluded from mainstream society. In other words, for the current Chinese government, tying all populations together by the belief in a myth of a common history is more important than addressing ethnic particularities and diversities. Sharing things in common, therefore, becomes an everlasting theme in the representation [construction] of ethnic minorities. The historiography of ethnic minorities was thus defined. Even today, after ethnic tourism has become a flourishing industry and a way to make money in several places, all representations about ethnic minorities, no matter whether they are in museums, theme parks, TV programmes, or films, must emphasize this theme of commonality in the first place, even though the details of how issues of ethnicity are presented may be different from those of the past in some aspects.

However, at least till the 1980s there were two points noteworthy in the official agreement about how to present or represent ethnic minorities: the position of each separate minority nationality in the genealogy of the social development/evolution of human beings, and the status of each separate minority nationality as a component part of the Chinese nation: zhonghua minzu. The former was the main goal of the investigation of ethnic minorities' social history, as discussed above. As to the latter, an official document, located in Fujian Provincial Archive dated back to 1958, titled 'Referential Outline of the She Nationality Investigation' provides a good example. In this outline things regarded as cultural in ethnology are not important to the investigation. Although this outline was at that time drafted on behalf of the investigation into the She people, 'it could also be referential for investigating Hui and Man nationalities' (FPA: 138-2-887, 17). It basically covers the main data and information that the project investigating ethnic minorities' social history was looking for. With more than 10,000 characters in length, this outline devotes only an insignificant portion to cultural events. The outline is divided into the following sections: (1) instruction, (2) ethnic origin (minzu qiyuan), (3) ethnic history (minzu lishi), (4) political situation (zhengzhi qingkuang), (5) economy, (6) changes in living customs, (7) religious beliefs, (8) cultural education and hygiene (wenhua jiaoyu yu weisheng), (9) interethnic relations, and (10) the circumstance of the Great Leap Forward in Socialist Construction (shehui zhuyi jianshe dayuejin qingkuang).

Apart from 1, 2, 6, and 7, all the other topics/subjects are associated with very detailed and specific requirements of the data collection, regarding the materials that ideological propaganda would need. For example, the outline emphasizes gathering the data in terms of these issues: She revolutionary history, their relations of production, class struggle, etc. Under each of these topics there are many more elaborate categories. For instance, in Sections 2 and 3, the investigation has to focus on how important the She have been as part of the Chinese nation and how the She have been involved in making contributions to the Chinese nation. Item 4 asks for the provision of data in terms of how the She people has participated in different popular revolutions throughout history, especially their participation in the Chinese communist revolution. In Section 5, data on how the She people were exploited and suppressed over time under the 'three big mountains' (imperialism, feudalism, and bureaucratic capitalism) is required. The topic of 'exploitation through land rents' (dizu boxue), which is included in Section 5 of the outline, specifies the investigation into different forms of rent, such as labour rent, rent in kind, or money rent, in particular. In addition to such specific categories, the outline also lists a number of technical questions, regarding the deposits required for rent, sharecropping or fixed rent, and the ratio of average rent to yield per mu, among many other details. The investigators are asked to collect data and information about how great a change the party-state has brought to the social life of the She. Section 9 is under the rubric of interethnic relations, so that the investigation has to specify the relations between the She and their neighboring Han over time and especially how such relations had been improved after the liberation in 1949. What's more, in Section 10, the outline demands that investigators should emphasize how changes took place in every aspect of She social and political lives after 1949 and how they had passionately participated in the great-socialist construction. Based on this outline, a book, The Concise History of the She Nationality (Shezu Jianshi), came out later (Bianxiezu 2009 [1978]).

The above example shows that those phenomena regarded as ethnic markers, most of which are cultural, were not important to the authorities in their consideration of minority issues. First, cultural differences among ethnic minorities were taken for granted; so, it was needless to pay them any particular attention. Second, having pretended to be the messianic deliverer (see Kornai 1992), what the party-state mostly wanted was proof of the work it had done, which they presumed was that it had rescued the minority people from an abyss of suffering.

The data collected through the social history project had to be sorted out to fit into the Marxist five-stage-model of social development in order to establish a hierarchical structure, in which each separate minority nationality would have its social position congruent with the stages of primitive, slave, or feudal society, by the time of 'democratic reform' (minzhu gaige). Analysis of the relations of production was applied to the study of every separate minority nationality for determination of their positions in this hierarchical evolutionary structure. Not surprisingly one finds that, in the outline provided above, Sections 4 and 5, 'Political Situation' and 'Economy' occupy a great portion of the contents. The projects of minority work (identification and social history projects mainly) resulted in five series of publications (wutao congshu) and the publications included in three of them, namely the historiographies of each minority nationality (shaoshu minzu zhi), the concise histories of each minority nationality, and the concise ethnographies of each minority nationality, all defined in terms of what stage of social development a minority nationality had reached, before the 'democratic reform'. The Yi, as a newly constructed minority nationality, cover in fact several different ethnic groups in the southwest; some of them who lived in the Great and Small Cool Mountains in Sichuan and Yunnan were defined being as at a 'slave society' stage; several hunting and gathering groups in the northeast and southwest were defined as still at the stage of 'primitive society'. Tibetan society was defined as a 'feudal serfdom' (fengjian nongnuzhi), which was considered to be one of the earlier forms of feudal society, which itself was considered to be the final stage before the capitalist one.

Today, such a linear line of progress, or evolution, or social development has come to shape the minds of ordinary people. As have mentioned the Jingpo (Kachin) are a minority nationality whose stage of social development was defined as one of late primitive society, according to their system of ownership and level of productivity. After the ' democratic reform' and Land Reform in the 1950s, however, they were also considered as a people who needed urgent help to bring them to 'directly pass over' (zhijie guodu or zhiguo) several stages prior to the stage of the socialist society in order to reach it (Ma 1999). Ironically, the term zhiguo has since become a name used by the local Han and Dai for the Jingpo and has even been accepted by Jingpo people themselves as well. Because zhiguo implies 'backward', especially by comparison with both the Han and the Dai in the locality, the decades-long use of the term since it was first coined has caused the Jingpo people to feel psychologically abused and therefore inferior. It has become a matter of everyday sensitivity among the Jingpo especially when they encounter either Han or Dai people. What's more, in the past, shantou ('mountaintop') was a term used by local people to call the Jingpo who traditionally lived in the mountains. Calling them Shantou was not meant to insult them but to differentiate them from those minority people who have traditionally lived by the waters such as the Dai. However, nowadays shantou has become an insulting term to the Jingpo people since it has come to mean stupid, ignorant, and isolated (Yu 2010, 17–18). These cases show how the peoples themselves have cognitively internalize the linear-hierarchical model of social development.

The categorization of population in this way and the listing all the categories in a particular order in accordance with a lineal-hierarchical structure of social evolution essentially put all minorities in a situation opposed to the advocacy of interethnic equality, the promise the CCP had made to ethnic minorities while engaged in the revolution. The CCP admits the inequality among nationalities in terms of their social development but has never recognized that the ways in which the communists understood minority issues would actually create a new kind of inequality. This conception of an inherent inequality in social development by the CCP resulted in an authoritative empowering of the Han and others considered more advanced nationalities, since the inequalities of social development needed to be evened out and the Han were considered to be the most advanced of all peoples in China. The Han, therefore, have a responsibility to help the ethnic minorities in every aspect so that the majority can share a common development (gongtong fazhan) with their ethnic minority brothers. The discourse of interethnic brotherhood that the party-state propaganda machine has produced has long dominated official expectations of interethnic relationships. It was supposed to bring those who had been excluded from mainstream society together, since what was 'advanced' and what was 'backward' was defined by neither culture nor race but by the level of social development that was considered politically correct then, according to the party-state. Thus, contrary to what Herzfeld (2005) argues, in the conceptualization of Chinese nation, the kinship metaphors, such as brotherhood, are constructed through ranking one another according to its position on the road of social evolution rather than claiming to share something primordially the same.

The discourse of interethnic brotherhood has been aimed at implementing the state's nation-building programme. The statement, 'China has been a unified, multiple national state since its ancient times', may have come about much earlier. However, it was first officially announced only during the preparations for the tenth anniversary of the establishment of the PRC. Nowadays, except for a few cases, most ethnic minorities have no objection to the ethnic categories the state has assigned to them, and most of them also hold on to an identity as a member of the Chinese nation. The term minzu (the term the Chinese use for a wide array of terms such as nation, people, ethnic group, etc.) has concealed the meaning of statehood within the notion of 'nation'. In conjunction with state policy towards national minorities, a new kind of nationalism has constructed a national identity for them. It is not hard to see that some of the most radical meanings of nationalism or patriotism are conveyed by the writings of authors of different minority nationalities, although their strong sense of being Chinese nationals may manifest itself in attacks on Han chauvinism.

Consequently, any representation related to any minority nationality in China today, even those that are produced in order to respond to waves of tourism or other forms of cultural commercialism in recent years, has to start with some description of the importance or the position of the ethnic minority in the course of the creation of the Chinese nation throughout history. A separate nationality could not be legitimately presented without this precondition. As a whole, the legitimacy of any particular nationality must be expressed or reified within the general discourse of the Chinese nation. The subjectivity of the people of a separate nationality was thus to be recognized or defined only in these terms. Logically, a narrative style like this is similar to that of a Chinese genealogy in which a family history starts with a phrase such as Guo you guo shi, jia you jia cheng (a country should have its historiography whereas a family should have its genealogy). To obtain recognition from outside a Chinese descent group had to establish a link to some higher power. In the same way, a minority nationality in China can only have its legitimacy recognized through joining in the family of the Chinese nation. However, the members in this family form a lineal-hierarchical structure. The 'past' was spatially manifested in the present in the way through which modernism typically creates its 'others' – such as the traditional, primitive, savage, or barbarian – for the purposes of defining modernity. In the Chinese context, the party-state used notions of 'advanced' and 'backward', a synchronic embodiment of the chronological, to create these others so to include all of them within the construction of a Chinese nation, in which all different groups of peoples become brothers, at least, in theory.

Conclusion

Unlike the construction of more alien cultural others in representations of cultural encounters in Western countries (Hallam and Street 2000), the representation of ethnic minorities in China after 1949 and before the 1980s had to a great extent dismissed the cultural particularities of its subjects. Such a representation was produced through a top-down process, conveying the will of the party-state. It has served to emphasize commonality, producing meanings that would serve the purpose of constructing Zhonghua Minzu, the Chinese nation. If, as Asad (2000) claims, in the construction of European identity, Muslims 'are included within and excluded from Europe at one and the same time', the construction of the identity of the new Chinese nation must be manifested through absorbing the specific ethnic identities that Chinese civilization had traditionally excluded. Therefore, in all representations of ethnic minorities or for the purposes of representing a cosmopolitan Chinese history, gongtong dizhao (to co-create or co-construct) has become the most important theme.

In sum, based on the ethnic identification campaign and the project of investigating social history of ethnic minorities that took place in the 1950s, ways of representation of ethnic minorities and a systematic body of knowledge about the minority people were established. Except for the ten years of the Cultural Revolution (1966–1976), the government and academia have never stopped researches among ethnic minorities. Most of these investigations and researches still follow the themes set up during the 1950s (although they may be contradicted to some extent by the new emphasis on cultural particularity in the media and ethnic parks). If the campaign of ethnic identification was a component part of state-making (Fan 2012), the investigation of ethnic minorities' social histories and its consequent works and results, then, were associated with the engineering of nation-building of the Chinese nation. In recent decades, however, representation of ethnic minorities have gradually shifted away from stages of social development to cultural matters, albeit in line with a constructed Chinese nation in terms of narrative, in an increasingly globalized China.

Acknowledgements

The earliest version of this paper was presented to *International Workshop on Minority Groups in China and the U.S.* Tufts University, Boston, USA, 25–27 June 2010. I would like to express thanks to Professors Nathan Glazer, Reed Ueda, and Ma Rong, the organizers of the workshop, who invited and funded me to attend. I am extremely grateful to three anonymous reviewers for their constructive comments and suggestions. My thanks especially go to Professors Michael Dillon and Thomas Simon. Not only has Professor Dillom invited me to join this issue but also offered helps when I was completing this article. Professor Simon's insightful comments have made this paper a lot more readable.

Disclosure statement

No potential conflict of interest was reported by the author.

Funding

This work was supported by the National Foundation for Philosophy and Social Sciences, Peoples' Republic of China [grant number 09AMZ001].

References

Anagnost, Ann. 1997. *National Past-Times: Narrative, Representation, and Power in Modern China*. Durham, NC: Duke University Press.
Anderson, Benedict. 1998. *The Spectre of Comparisons: Nationalism, Southeast Asia and the World*. London: Verso.
Asad, Talal. 2000. "Muslims and European Identity: Can Europe Represent Islam?" In *Cultural Encounters: Representing Otherness*, edited by Elizabeth Hallam and Brian Street, 11–28. London: Routledge.
Bianxiezu (writing group). 2009 [1978]. *Shezu Jianshi [The Concise History of the She Nationality]*. Beijing: Minzu Chubanshe.
Chatterjee, Partha. 2004. *The Politics of the Governed*. New York: Columbia University Press.

Chen, Guoqiang. 1999. "Huiyi Fujiansheng Shaoshuminzu Shehui Lishi Diaocha [Recollection of Minority Nationalities' Social History Investigation in Fujian Province]." In *Tianye Diaocha Shilu—Minzu Diaocha Huiyi [Memoir of Field Investigation: Recollections from Investigation of Ethnic Minorities]*, edited by Hao Shiyuan, Ren Yifei and Shi Lianzhu, 347–354. Beijing: Shehui Kexue Wenxian Chubanshe.

Chen, Jie. 2008. "Nation, Ethnicity, and Cultural Strategies: Three Waves of Ethnic Representation in Post-1949." Ph.D. Dissertation, The State University of New Jersey, New Brunswick, NJ.

Elias, Norbert. 1994. *Reflection on a Life*. Cambridge: Polity Press.

Elias, Norbert. 1998. *On Civilization, Power, and Knowledge*. Chicago, IL: University of Chicago Press.

Fan, Ke. 2012. "Ethnic Configuration and State Making: A Fujian Case." *Modern Asian Studies* 46 (4): 915–945.

Fan, Ke. 2015. *Zaiye de Quanqiuhua: Liudong, Xinren yu Rentong [Globalization at Large: Mobility, Trust and Identity]*. Beijing: Zhishi Chanquan Chubanshe.

Fiskesjö, Magus. 2015. "Wa Grotesque: Headhunting Theme Parks and the Chinese Nostalgia for Primitive Contemporaries." *Ethnos: Journal of Anthropology* 80 (4): 497–523.

Foucault, M. 2000. "Governmentality." In Power, edited by James D. Faubion, 239–297. New York: New Press.

Giddens, Anthony. 1990. *The Consequences of Modernity*. Stanford, CA: Stanford University Press.

Gladney, Dru. 1994. "Representing Nationality in China: Refiguring Majority/Minority Identities." *The Journal of Asian Studies* 53 (1): 92–123.

Hall, Stuart. 2003. "Introduction." In *Representation: Cultural Representations and Signifying Practices*, edited by Stuart Hall, 1–12. London: Sage Publication.

Hallam, Elizabeth, and Brian Street. 2000. "Introduction: Cultural Encounters-Representing "Otherness'." In *Cultural Encounters: Representing "Otherness"*, edited by Elizabeth Hallam and Brian Street, 1–10. London: Routledge.

Harrell, Stevan. 1995. "Introduction: Civilizing Projects and the Reaction to Them." In *Cultural Encounters in China's Ethnic Frontiers*, edited by Stevan Harrell, 22–44. Seattle: University of Washington Press.

Herzfeld, Michael. 2005. *Cultural Intimacy: Social Poetics in the Nation-State*. New York: Routledge.

Huang, Guangxue, and Lianzhu Shi, eds. 2005. *Zhongguo de Minzu Shibie [Ethnic Identification in China]*. Beijing: Minzu Chubanshe.

Kornai, J'anos. 1992. *Socialist System: The Political Economy of Communism*. Princeton, NJ: Princeton University Press.

Ma, Yao. 1999. "Ji Jianguo Chuqi de Yunnan Minzu Diaocha" [Investigating Ethnic Minorities in Yunnan in the Early Period of the PRC]." In *Tianye Diaocha Shilu— Minzu Diaocha Huiyi [Memoir of Field Investigation: Recollections from Investigation of Ethnic Minorities]*, edited by Hao Shiyuan, Ren Yifei and Hua Zugen, 1–16. Beijing: Shehui Kexue Wenxian Chubanshe.

Postiglione, Gerard A. 1999. "Introduction: State Schooling and Ethnicity in China." *China's National Minority Education: Culture, Schooling and Development*, edited by Gerard A. Postiglione, 3–20. New York: Falmer Press.

Tapp, Nicolas C. T. 2002. "Engendering the "Miao': Belonging and the Marginal." *Bulletin of the Department of Anthropology*. No. 58: 59–77.

Varutti, Marzia. 2011. "Miniatures of the Nation: Ethnic Minority Figurines, Mannequins and Dioramas in Chinese Museums." *Museum & Society* 9 (1): 1–16.

Vickers, Edward. 2007. "Museums and Nationalism in Contemporary China." *Compare: A Journal of Comparative and International Education* 37 (3): 365–382.

Yu, Li. 2000. "Representation of Ethnic Minorities in Chinese Propaganda Posters, 1957–1983." Modern Chinese Literature and Culture (MCLC) Resource Center Publication. http://mclc.osu.edu/rc/pubs/minzu/.

Yu, Xiaoyan. 2010. "Xingzou zai Bianyuan: Yunnan Chengzizheng de Cunyi Zhiye Bianqian [Walking in the Margin: Changes in the Village Doctors's Career in Changzi Township, Yunnan]." PhD diss., Department of Sociology, Tsinghua University, Beijing.

Zhao, Z., and G. A. Postiglione. 2010. "Representations of Ethnic Minorities in China's University Media." *Discourse: Studies in the Cultural Politics of Education* 31 (3): 319–334.

More Islamic, no less Chinese: explorations into overseas Chinese Muslim identities in Malaysia

Chow Bing Ngeow[a] and Hailong Ma[b]

[a]Institute of China Studies, University of Malaya, Kuala Lumpur, Malaysia; [b]Department of Anthropology, Sun Yat-sen University, Guangzhou, People' s Republic of China

ABSTRACT
This paper explores the newly emerging overseas Chinese Muslim community in Malaysia. As China's interactions with the Muslim-majority countries deepen, there will be more Chinese Muslims staying in these countries. Questions can be asked how connection with, and exposure to, the wider Islamic world influence their identity as Chinese Muslim. Through examining the activities of the Overseas Chinese Muslim Association, elite interviews and survey data of the Chinese Muslim students in Malaysia, this paper argues that in general overseas Chinese Muslims remain comfortable with their identity as both Muslim and Chinese. Some contributing factors include the presence of a sizable ethnic Chinese minority in Malaysia and the ease of modern communications technology. They also utilize their different identity categories to maximize advantages to the community. Also, the Chinese Muslims' relations with official China and the Han majority are largely reproduced in Malaysia.

As China embarks on its ambitious strategy of 'One Belt One Road' (the Silk Road Economic Belt and the twenty-first century Maritime Silk Road), it is likely that China's interaction with the Muslim world will intensify, as many countries along the 'Belt' and the 'Road' are Muslim-majority countries. Muslims in China therefore will become the potential facilitators and bridge builders for the Chinese state in this geopolitical and geoeconomic task. As Ho (2013) perceptively argues, there is an increased strategic importance of the Muslim minorities to the Chinese state, and the state is keen to mobilize them in its dealings with Muslim-majority countries. The Chinese Muslim minority groups in the process also increase their leverage and advantages vis-à-vis the state. Increasingly also, more and more Muslims from China will become students, workers, professionals, businesspersons in these Muslim-majority countries. Even before the recent pronouncement of 'One Belt One Road', overseas Chinese Muslim communities are increasingly more common in countries such as Turkey, Indonesia, Egypt, United Arab Emirates, Malaysia, and others. These 'overseas Chinese Muslims' differ from the traditional conception of Chinese diaspora or Chinese overseas. This is a phenomenon that has not been widely studied in the academic world.

This paper is a preliminary examination of the identities of overseas Chinese Muslim community in Malaysia. Three conceptual issue need to be clarified first. First, this paper focuses on those Chinese Muslims who ventured out from China since the 1980s and 1990s, after the opening-up and reform of China in the late 1970s, and most of them are still holders of the citizenship of the People's Republic of China (PRC). In this sense, they are not the same with the ethnic Chinese citizens of other countries who are Muslims.

Second, this paper necessarily uses 'Chinese Muslims' as an inclusive term to cover all Muslim ethnic groups in China (Uyghur, Hui, Dongxiang, etc.), although overwhelmingly the Chinese Muslims whom the authors encountered throughout this research are Hui Muslims. There are two reasons that the term is being used in a broad sense as to include non-Hui Chinese Muslims. First, some of the respondents to a survey we administered do not belong to the Hui ethnic group. Second, the organization that these Chinese Muslims set up for themselves in Malaysia is indeed called 'Overseas Chinese Muslim Association (OCMA)' and is meant to be inclusive of all Chinese Muslim ethnic groups, not just the Hui, even though almost all members of this organization are of Hui ethnicity. An unknown number of Uyghurs also reside in Malaysia; many of them stay outside of public scrutiny and cannot be reached easily, hence the conclusion from this paper cannot be generalized to the Uyghur Muslims.

Finally, 'identity' here means a social or group identity, that is, an individual membership in a larger category in which the individual subjectively either identifies with, or objectively is being identified with by others, or both. These categories can be based on various sorts of typologies, including gender, race, class, religion, and so forth. An individual is unlikely to hold only one group identity at the expense of all the others, but there are always circumstances or factors that result in the individual exploring how to adjust, elevate, or abandon, one of his/her group identities, such as migration.

This paper is divided into seven sections. The first section situates the analysis of this transnational community in the context of three bodies of academic literature. The second section introduces the history of the overseas Chinese Muslim community in Malaysia. The third section reports on the formation and activities of the OCMA. The fourth section covers two interviews of the influential members of this Muslim community. The fifth section reports the findings of a survey. The sixth section offers theoretical discussion. The final section offers reflections and conclusion.

Overseas Chinese ethnic minorities, Chinese Muslims and China, and identities in transnationalism

By focusing on this distinct group of Chinese, the analysis and implications of this paper can be situated within three groups of academic literature: the studies of overseas Chinese (especially the overseas Chinese ethnic minorities), the studies of Chinese Muslims and China, and the studies of identity in the context of transnationalism.

Overseas Chinese ethnic minorities

Critiquing the western anthropological and historical scholarship on Chinese minority and overseas Chinese, Vasantkumar faults none of them

> capture the strangeness of the … situation, for Chinese-ness as it is studied today is simultaneously many and one –many within the PRC and one without. Within the People's Republic, a 'unified multi-ethnic state,' Chinese-ness is formally plural … Outside of the PRC, however … one finds an Overseas Chinese-ness that is geographically unbounded and resolutely uniform in ethno-racial terms –one identity instead of fifty-six. (Vasantkumar 2012, 426)

Scholars within China have realized this 'strangeness' and the subfield of 'Studies of Overseas Chinese Ethnic Minorities' (*shaoshu minzhu huaqiao huaren yanjiu*) has developed. Chinese scholars tend to focus on definitional issues, population estimation, and causes of the outmigration of the minority people (Zhao 2004). The fact that many of these overseas Chinese ethnic minorities left China because of the fear (and fact) of suppression or discrimination by the Han majority also underscored a policy significance for the government of the PRC for this academic field – in terms of consolidating the overseas Chinese ethnic minorities' positive identification with the Chinese state (or at least positive perception of or connection with the PRC if they have become citizens of other states) and with the Chinese Nation (*Zhonghua minzu*, which in official rhetoric consists of the Han majority and the 55 officially recognized ethnic minorities). Such *problematique*, however, invites criticism. Barabantseva's study of the official policy and scholarly discourse on 'overseas Chinese ethnic minorities', for example, criticizes this field for it 'is an expression of sovereign power directed at the creation of transnational identities that ultimately emphasize unity and cohesion over diversity within the Chinese nation' (Barabantseva 2012, 99).

Among the 'overseas Chinese ethnic minorities', the Chinese Muslims maintained one of the largest overseas communities outside of China. The largest Muslim ethnic group is the Hui, followed by the Uyghurs, and together, they comprise about 20 million out of the 22 million Muslims in China. Both groups have substantial transnational networks. Unlike the Chinese diaspora, the Uyghur diaspora was formed to resist and severe ties with China and for the purpose of creating an independent state. The scholarly attention on the Hui Muslim diaspora tends to focus on the 'Dungans' (or Donggan Ren in Mandarin) in Central Asia. These 'Chinese-speaking Muslims' came to central Asia (today's Kazakhstan, Kyrgyzstan, and Uzbekistan) escaping Imperial Qing's oppression of the Hui in the nineteenth century. Soviet scholars were the first to take notice of them, followed by western and PRC scholars (Allès 2005).

Other than the Uyghurs and the Dungans, studies of Chinese Muslims outside of China are sporadic at best. Some of these studies are macro-level overviews, detailing historical periods and demographics of the Chinese Muslim diaspora (Ma 2005a; Liang 2012),[1] while others focusing on the issues faced by Chinese Muslim communities (such as employment patterns, state's policies, identities) in countries such as Canada, Indonesia, and Malaysia (Ma 2005a, 2005b; Muzakki 2010; Wong, 2013; Hew 2014; Chen 2015). Except for Wong's article, none of them deals with the overseas Chinese Muslims who ventured out since the late 1970s – the focus of this paper.

Wong's paper, however, does not specifically deal with the identity issue of these overseas Chinese Muslims in Malaysia, which this paper attempts to illuminate. This is also pertinent to the larger and more voluminous literature grappling with the concerns of the identity of the Muslim ethnic groups in China.

Chinese Muslims and China

As Dru Gladney points out, two contrasting views inform the relationship between Muslims and the Chinese socio-political order: accommodation and separatism (Gladney 2003). While in general the Hui are culturally similar to the Han and more accommodative to their minority status, the Uyghurs in general are resistant of Han Chinese rule. However, beyond this simple dichotomy are the wide differences within each Muslim ethnic group as well. The Hui identity is a product of the dialogic and interactive process between state's categorization and the Hui people's appropriation of such category (Gladney 1996). Lipman similarly is sceptical of the overarching 'Hui' identity and notes that different localities have an important role to play – in interlocking interaction with the 'ethnicization' process coming from the state – in the formation of the Hui identities (Lipman 2004).

Instead of looking at the 'localization' factor, this paper examines the impact of the opposite: the 'globalization' factor. As Gladney has suggested, since the reform era, the state's generally permissive attitude towards expression of the ethnic and religious identity of the Hui, together with the advent of modern communications technology, is connecting or reconnecting the Hui with the larger Islamic world (Gladney 1996, 326–328). The exposure to Islamic internationalism, as Gladney suggests, will make traditional Hui identities 'once again be reshaped and called into question, giving rise to new manifestations of Islam in China' (Gladney 2003: 463). Pursuing this line of inquiry, a series of questions can be asked: How will the connection with the wider Muslim world affect the Chinese Muslims? Will their dual identity as Chinese and Muslim be confirmed, redefined, or challenged when they are exposed to a predominantly Islamic culture? If, as suggested by Raphael Israeli, that Muslim communities in China have maintained and enhanced their consciousness of the Islamic *umma* (universal community) 'by cultivating in the Muslim the centrality of Arabia, Islam, and the Islamic Empire, and Islamic traditions and values', and that they see 'China [as] not the fatherland of the Hui nationality' (cited in Robinson 1994, 216), will not greater connection with the Muslim world reinforce their sense of cohesion with the coreligionists outside of China and of alienation from the Chinese heritage? The 'globalization' factor will become increasingly important in examining the identity issue of the Chinese Muslims. This in turn is tied to the theoretical literature examining identity in a transnational context.

Identities and transnationalism

Transnationalism was an emerging field in the 1990s. It grew because the traditional focus of migration studies or diaspora studies (with heavy emphasis on processes such as acculturation, assimilation, or multiculturalism) was deemed to be inadequate for understanding phenomena such as circulatory mobility, migrants' constant contacts with the sending-country societies, deterritorialized imagination of ethnic community, cultural reproduction and hybridity reinforced by constant cross-border flows of symbols and values, the emergence of travel and communication technologies that intensify transnational ties, and so on.

It is with this context of transnationalism that we examine the issue of identity. As mentioned earlier, there are both objective and subjective aspects of identity. A primordialist understanding of identity focuses on the objective aspects of identity and how these aspects continue to be emotionally important; since these objective aspects are likely inherited, primordialists also tend to argue that there is very little likelihood of changes of the social identity of an individual, and stress the enduring power of ethnonationalism (Isaacs 1975).

In contrast, constructivist theories of identity emphasize the subjective aspect. Identity henceforth is not something assumed to be inherited; instead, there are always possibilities for the processes of construction and reconstruction of identity. They are being shaped and negotiated through a dialectical (internally self-attributed and external ascribed) process, where the 'other' is usually as crucial as the self in determining one's identity (Vertovec 2001: 573). The instrumentalist or rational choice variant of constructivism focuses on the rational incentives and payoffs to the individuals in the adoption and construction of different identities (Laitin 1998).

Other constructivists analyse the role of the state in imposing or hegemonic role in legitimating or de-legitimating identities. In the case of the identities of transnational groups, often, they are conditioned by the power of at least two states (the sending and recipient states). The state's policies and ideologies have varying form of influences in the formation of identities, ranging from those imposing national homogeneity and purity to those more permissive of expression of different identities. Hence, Danforth's study of the Macedonians (and by extension the diaspora originated from the conflict-prone Balkan) in western democracies suggests that identity construction is

> influenced by hegemonic constructions that have their origins in both the countries where they were born and the countries where they have settled … [and] for those whose identities were denied in their homelands, the most salient feature of the politics of identity in the diaspora is the fact that they now enjoy the freedom to express an identity.

Individuals who had been without a national identity, now had 'come to acquire a sense of national identity', possible under a transnational context (Danforth 1995, 200–202).

In this paper, will the different socio-political environments (China and Malaysia) experienced by these transnational Chinese Muslims in Malaysia affect their views on their own identities? When they come to Malaysia, will 'Chinese' remain a national, ethnic, or cultural category? While in Malaysia, Islam has been socially largely conflated with an ethnic category (Malay), how will the Chinese Muslims respond to this social environment? By researching the overseas Chinese Muslims, this paper advances the understanding of how an ethnic minority group manages the coexistence of different identity categories (Muslim and Chinese) in a transnational context.

Overseas Chinese Muslim community in Malaysia

When Chinese Muslim students decided to seek education abroad, their choice of countries usually differs from the choices made by non-Muslim Chinese students. In the late Qing and Republican eras, many Chinese students went to Japan or the West, but for Chinese Muslim intellectuals and students, their focus was to establish ties with institutions in the Muslim world, such as Al Azhar University in Egypt (Yao 1999). In the post-Mao era, Chinese students again emerged in Western countries and Japan. Again,

Chinese Muslim students' options for foreign education differed from the non-Muslim students. In 1982, China Islamic Association sponsored 10 Chinese Muslim students to study at Al Azhar, renewing an academic relationship that had been absent for more than thirty years under Maoist rule (Ma and Yang 1988: 127). In the 1990s, a Sino-Arabic school in Linxia (Gansu province) sent 46 students to countries such as Pakistan, Saudi Arabia, Syria, Sudan, India, and Malaysia (Xie, Shu, and Ma 2002: 157), which generally would not prompt the interests of the non-Muslim Chinese students.

Two factors shaped the choice of these Muslim students seeking higher education abroad. First, in the domestic institutions of higher learning in China, even among those that cater for ethnic minorities, significant (perceived or real) constraints for the Chinese Muslim students still persist (Zhao 2014). Second, as Chinese Muslim students mostly come from the interior provinces of China and tend to have lower socio-economic status compared to the Han students in coastal areas, they tend not to be able to afford the higher education in the more prosperous countries in the developed world. Henceforth, obtaining a foreign education in Muslim countries has been a preferred option for those who can afford.

Formation of the overseas Chinese Muslim community in Malaysia

It was within this context that Malaysia saw the arrival of Muslim students from China. This began in the late 1980s and early 1990s, where a small group of Hui Muslim students from China started attending Malaysia's International Islamic University (Universiti Islam Antarabangsa, abbreviated as UIA), which was then providing some financial subsidies for these Chinese students.

An important organization that played a role in bringing Muslim students from China was Regional Islamic Da'wah Council of Southeast Asia and the Pacific (RISEAP). It is a government-supported non-governmental organization based in Kuala Lumpur, with the mission to connect Muslim minorities in different countries of the region, and to preach Islam to non-Muslim people. In 1982, President of RISEAP, Tunku Abdul Rahman (who was the first Prime Minister of Malaysia from 1957 to 1970) led the first RISEAP delegation to visit China, under the invitation of China Islamic Association (RISEAP 1982). In July 1988 and September–October 1995, RISEAP sent two more delegations to China (RISEAP 1988, 1995), with the agenda of cooperation in education that resulted in opening up Malaysian institutions of higher education to Chinese Muslim students, as mentioned above.

Towards the late 1990s, Chinese Muslim students numbered about a hundred. A significant number of them stayed in Malaysia after graduation, to continue studies, do business, or work. They also became the local contacts for the interested and incoming Chinese Muslim students in the coming years.

This was the beginning of the overseas Chinese Muslim community studied in this paper. Today, it can be roughly estimated that there are about 200–300 families of this community who are residing in Malaysia on a long-term basis, while other mobile (circulatory) students and businesspersons are also part of this community. They are based in several locales, spread wide across in peninsular Malaysia, in the states of Selangor, Terengganu, Kedah, and Kelantan, but mostly in the Gombak district in Selangor (where the main campus of UIA is located), about 20 km north of the capital city Kuala Lumpur. Apart from the sizable Chinese Muslim student population at UIA, many restaurants opened by Chinese Muslims are concentrated in Gombak as well, as are some of their textile, tourism, and educational exchange businesses. In addition, Gombak is also where the headquarters of OCMA is located. Gombak therefore serves as a kind of geographical centre of this community. OCMA is the newly established organization (in 2012) to represent and articulate the interests of these overseas Chinese Muslims. OCMA is different from the Malaysian Chinese Muslim Association (MACMA), which is the organization of the ethnic Chinese Malaysian citizens who are Muslims.

Overseas Chinese Muslim association

OCMA maintains a website (http://muslimcn.org) that chronicles its formation and activities, some of which was directly participated and observed by a co-author of this paper, who has been a member of this association. The below information is drawn from OCMA's website as well as the field research note from the said author.

From its very beginning the transnational character of OCMA was shown, in which it states that it is to service the Chinese Muslims from China, including students, those who have settled in Malaysia for work or business, and those who come back and forth between China and Malaysia. According to an interviewed leader of OCMA (see below), in its early stage of formation, OCMA also received assistance from MACMA, with some overlapping of personnel, but gradually, it became an exclusive organization for the citizens of PRC. OCMA's relationship with MACMA remained cordial, but there has been less interaction lately.

From its website, it can be seen that OCMA has been relatively active in participating in Islam-related activities and events organized by the Malaysian government, such as 'Quranic' recitation contests or visits to mosques. On its own, it is active in some kind of Islamic transnational activism, such as showing support for the Palestinians and the Rohingya people. What is notable is the relative absence of significant activities that had any connection with official China. OCMA is registered in Malaysia and has cultivated ties with the official side of Malaysia extensively; however, it does not have many relations (if at all) with the Chinese embassy in Malaysia, unlike other organizations formed by PRC's citizens in Malaysia (such as the China Enterprises

Association in Malaysia or the Malaysian Association of China Students and Alumni).

On the other hand, it is also clear that OCMA maintains extensive transnational ties with the Muslims in China. It sent a large delegation to China's National Hui Conference in Quanzhou in 2012. Occasionally, OCMA also plays the role of connecting Muslim businesses between China and Malaysia and serves as a facilitator for Malaysian Halal Industry to expand in the Chinese market. However, in 2015, there was another newly formed organization called the Malaysia-China Muslim Chamber of Commerce, led actually by a sitting vice president of OCMA, which purportedly wishes to specialize in building up the business ties between Muslims businesses in China and Malaysia.

In December 2014–January 2015, the east coast of peninsular Malaysia experienced the worst flood in 30 years. Residents affected by the flood were predominantly Malay-Muslims. OCMA mobilized its members and networks in China, appealing to the Chinese Muslims in both Malaysia and China (including a Muslim-based chamber of commerce in Yiwu, a city in Zhejiang province known for its sizable Muslim population) to help their 'Muslim' brothers and sisters, and successfully gathered donations from them, which amounted to about 100,000 Chinese Yuan. When OCMA sent the donations to the flood victims (in addition to more than 30 Chinese Muslim volunteers who helped in the relief work), they emphasized that such donations were from China. The Chinese embassy in Malaysia, which was also organizing another donation effort, was unaware of, or at least, not involved at all, with the efforts of these Chinese Muslims.

OCMA's extensive transnational ties with the Muslims in China have been facilitated mainly by the extensive use of modern communications technology. For instance, the online mobilization drive for donation to the Malaysian flood victims mentioned above was launched and coordinated mainly by Ganlandeng Internet Radio, which was also started by overseas Chinese Muslims in Malaysia. The appealing message to help the 'Muslim brothers and sisters' was spread mainly through weixin, the Chinese short message communication service. OCMA also maintains close relationship with Chinese Muslim Network (CMN), the largest Muslim-based online discussion forum in China. In February 2016, OCMA co-hosted a forum together with CMN with the theme of 'One Belt One Road, We are the First'. Although echoing Chinese leadership's initiative of 'One Belt One Road', the official presence in the forum was from the Malaysian side, including a senior official from the Tourism Ministry in Malaysia.

Interviews with elite members of the overseas Chinese Muslim community

A co-author of this paper conducted more than thirty in-depth interviews with Chinese Muslims from various walks of life in Malaysia since 2014. These interviews generally took one to three hours. Interview notes were prepared as transcripts afterwards. The selection of interviewees generally followed the 'snowballing tactic'. Due to the limits of space, we only present here two interviews with elite members of the community. In social science methodology, elite interviews are understood to be helpful in acquiring information from those who have access to specialized knowledge in certain social or political processes (Dexter 1970). The elites whom we interviewed were all highly educated, have a secure job, stay in Malaysia for a long time, and have some influence within the community, mostly through leadership positions in OCMA. As Laitin (1998, 23) observes, there are times when 'cultural entrepreneurs' of a community emerged to try to articulate for a change of identity or to naturalize or essentialize the status quo. The 'elites' here will be akin to the 'cultural entrepreneurs' mentioned by Laitin.

Mr C, entrepreneur

Mr C was a beneficiary of the 1995–98 RISEAP-JAKIM programme mentioned above. Today, he is a successful entrepreneur, with businesses in textile, catering, and property sectors. As a businessman, Mr C has extensive dealings with the two major ethnic groups in Malaysia (Malays and Chinese). 'Ninety percent of my business partners are Malays, and I am grateful to the Malays. For the Malaysian Chinese, I am full of admiration, they are more hardworking than other races', according to Mr C. Although the Malays share the same religion with him (all Malays are by definition Muslim in Malaysia), he also feels close to the predominantly non-Muslim (and descendants of Han) Malaysian Chinese as they share his language and culture. However, the community that he interacts with the most is still the Hui Muslims from China. As for the Han Chinese from China, Mr C admitted that there has been very little interaction except for some official businesses. He confirmed that his interactions with the Malaysian Chinese are even more extensive than interaction with the Han Chinese citizens from China. The relationship with the Chinese official side was also deliberately avoided, and was basically confined to China Islamic Association in Beijing, in which he was involved in some consultations regarding the Halal industry. It is clear that Mr C, and by extension, OCMA, felt the sense of being outside of the mainstream of China and being neglected by the Chinese embassy in Malaysia (which, to a certain extent, was the deliberate choice of the Chinese Muslims in Malaysia as well).

Being a foreign Muslim, Mr C found himself easily accepted by the Muslim-majority Malaysia, and also found that the religious thought and doctrine in Malaysia more 'progressive' (he did not specify what he meant) and aligned with international standard, and saw the quality of Chinese Islamic culture and worldview yet to catch up with those in Malaysia. He saw Malaysia as a modern and progressive Muslim country, and a better option for Chinese

Muslims to study or migrate compared to those of Middle Eastern countries. Still, he is quite adamant about his national and cultural identity as a Chinese. He is not interested in taking up Malaysian citizenship (a tough process on its own by the way, given Malaysia's strict process), although he does expect that his children will be granted citizenship. He has expressed delights in the growing strengths and influence of China. He views the economic exploits of the Hui Muslims as contributing to the growing economic strength of China as well. Mr C also insists that the cultural identity as a Chinese should not be lost. He prefers to send his children to the Chinese-language schools in Malaysia rather than the Malay-language schools (which certainly have more emphasis on Islamic religious education).

Mr M, academic

Mr M grew up in Northwestern China and majored in Chinese and Arabic languages in Northwestern Nationalities University and Peking University. He came to Malaysia in 1998, after studying Arabic in Saudi Arabia for three years between 1995 and 1998. Through a friend studying at that time at the Institutional of Islamic Thought and Civilization (ISTAC) at UIA in Malaysia, he knew about the Ph.D. programme under ISTAC and applied for it. Since 1998, he has been living in Malaysia for 17 years.

Mr M takes seriously the education of his daughters (all four of them). All of them are holders of PRC citizenship even if some of them were born in Malaysia. Like Mr C, he sent all of them to Chinese-language primary schools, which shows his desire to keep the cultural Chinese identity and not to be assimilated by the Malays, and in this sense, he is no different from the Malaysian Chinese in Malaysia. He said that even if he or his family were to take up Malaysian citizenship, the identification with the Chinese language and culture would not change. In his own words, 'a Hui is like a Han who embraces Islam', and there is too much 'Han DNA' within the Hui culture. For him, the Hui Muslims are in a unique position to 'sinicize Islam'. As he asserted to the authors, 'we Huis have our own culture. We tried to use Chinese concepts to interpret the Islamic faith and culture, and we are able to find concepts in the Chinese culture that are equivalent to the Islamic culture'. His sense of 'Chineseness' is displayed when he told the experience of filling out Malaysian's governmental forms, where questions regarding racial background were present. Mr M usually ticked the 'other' category but then wrote 'China Muslims' or 'China Hui Muslims', to distinguish himself (and his family) from the 'Chinese' category, yet wished to convey how he sees his own identity.

On the other hand, he laments the situation of the Muslim people in China, which he feels is deteriorating, and the blame does not go to the government's restrictive policies alone. He feels that the Chinese Muslims themselves are to blame for failing to take education (secular and religious education alike) seriously. He displays admiration for the Malaysian Chinese for their continued and steadfast support for the maintenance of Chinese education and culture within a political–social environment dominated by the Malays. There is a sense that he wishes the Chinese Muslims, as minorities in (the predominantly secular) China, to emulate the (predominantly non-Muslim) Malaysian Chinese minority in the Muslim-majority Malaysia, such as supporting their own education despite the strong reservation and objection from the government and the majority Malays about these Chinese minority-supported education institutions.

Survey of Chinese Muslim students

In this section, we present survey data of Chinese Muslim students pursuing higher education in Malaysia. Admittedly, the Chinese Muslim student population does not represent the whole overseas Chinese Muslim community. The survey sample also does not come from random sampling process. Instead, it was based on what Bryman termed as 'convenience sampling' (Bryman 2012, 201–202). As Bryman suggested, 'convenience sampling' is a legitimate research tool if is used as a first step towards a more scientific research design, or if it is a more practical way to gather information. Since it is too costly and impractical to draw a sample from the whole Chinese Muslim population in Malaysia at this stage, we have to opt for this more 'convenient' but less scientific way to gather some data. Therefore, the data presented here are only of supplementary nature. Still, we think that the survey data are useful, in the sense that the data can be contrasted with the elite interview data (between those who have just come to Malaysia and those who have stayed for much longer period), and that the data can also indicate the Chinese Muslim sense of identity during their initial stage of being exposed to a foreign, but Islamic, culture.

In February–June 2015, we carried out a survey of the Chinese Muslim students pursuing higher education in Malaysia, with 88 respondents (about 40 of them were collected from questionnaires, others collected from an online survey portal that was used by the authors). Because of the way the online survey portal was set up, respondents were able to ignore certain questions, hence the tables presented in this section will show varying sample size (N), although it can be seen that consistently around 73–75 respondents answered all the questions.

The survey questionnaire has 35 questions relating to population characteristics, educational experiences, religious experiences, and political and identity dimensions of these Chinese Muslim students in Malaysia. Here, we select and present data in the following tables from several questions that are more relevant to the discussion in this paper.

As can be seen from Table 1, not all respondents are Hui; there are at least three other non-Hui Chinese Muslim ethnic minorities, including one Ugyhur. However, the population body of Ugyhur Muslim students is definitely much larger, but they mostly stay outside of the contact of other Chinese Muslim students (and hence beyond our ability to reach this group). What is interesting to note here is that there are *Han* Chinese Muslims. They probably converted to Islam for a variety of reasons, such as seeking spiritual fulfilment. Table 2 confirms the picture whereby most Chinese Muslim students came from the interior or northwest provinces of China, significantly different from the Han Chinese diaspora that originated mostly from the coastal provinces.

As shown in Table 3, most of the surveyed students came to Malaysia not to study Islamic studies-related majors, which is somewhat surprising. A plurality of them concentrated on business and economic majors, which indicated an interest in business career after graduation. In this sense, they are not much different from most of the non-Muslim Chinese students. Nevertheless, the religious dimension of these overseas Chinese students is underscored in Tables 4–6, which show that they regard the learning of Islamic knowledge to be both an important factor to attract them to Malaysia and also an important element in their student life in Malaysia.

In addition to the questions regarding their religious life and experience, a series of questions are also designed to probe the respondents' perception and attitudes towards the political system and policies of both China and Malaysia; from here, the political and national identity of the respondents can be inferred to a certain extent. This series of questions is presented in Table 7.

As the table indicates, most respondents positively evaluated Malaysia's political system. In general, the categories of 'agree' and 'strongly agree' received much more agreement from the respondents compared to the categories of 'disagree' and 'strongly disagree' in appraising Malaysia 'as a democratic country', 'as an Islamic state', and 'as a secular state', although there might be inherent tensions among these three statements, especially from the viewpoints of non-Muslim minorities in Malaysia. Similarly, statements regarding Malaysia's Islamization trend and human rights records also received mostly positive answers ('agree' or 'strongly agree') from the

Table 1. Ethnicity.

Ethnicity	Number ($N = 88$)	Percentage
Hui	78	88.64
Han	5	5.68
Dongxiang	3	3.41
Uyghur	1	1.14
Salar	1	1.14

Table 2. Provincial origin.

Provincial Origin	Number (88)	Percentage
Ningxia	16	18.18
Xinjiang	14	15.91
Henan	13	14.77
Gansu	12	13.64
Yunnan	9	10.22
Qinghai	6	6.82
Shaanxi	3	3.41
Heilongjiang	3	3.41
Shanghai	2	2.27
Zhejiang	2	2.27
Hebei, Guangdong, Anhui, Inner Mongolia, Shanxi, Liaoning, Beijing and Tianjin	1 from each province	9.09

respondents, although the Islamization issue remains controversial and divisive in Malaysia precisely because of its potential impact on the human rights of Muslims and non-Muslims alike.

However, when it came to answering questions regarding China, respondents displayed a far more nuanced understanding. In response to appraising whether China 'is a 'democratic country', 'respects freedom of religion', and 'has satisfactory policy towards ethnic minorities', respondents who chose 'strongly disagree' and 'disagree' outnumbered those who chose 'agree' and 'strongly agree'. On the other hand, while displaying these disapproving attitudes towards the government of China, many respondents were, however, proud of their Chinese national identity as well. Overwhelmingly, many of them answered 'agree' or 'strongly agree' in affirming that Muslim ethnic groups belong to the one big family of *Zhonghua Minzu* (the Chinese Nation). They also agreed that China's territorial claims over some of the neighbouring countries are legitimate, and that overseas Chinese Muslims should promote Chinese culture.

Finally, a question in the questionnaire probes the respondents' intention to become Malaysian citizens. Malaysia maintains a strict and prohibitive naturalization procedure; therefore, the question was designed with the added phrase 'if conditions permitted' to try to get the sense of how much the respondents were willing to stay in a Muslim-majority country where their religious identity can be freely expressed or in the more tightly controlled environment of their homeland. Twenty-seven respondents answered

Table 3. Majors in universities.

Majors and disciplines	Number (N = 75)	Percentage
Economics and Business	35	46.67
Islam and Arabic	17	22.67
Humanities and Social Sciences	16	21.33
Science and Engineering	4	5.33
English	3	4

Table 4. Learning of Islamic knowledge.

Q: After coming to Malaysia, have you been continuing the learning of Islamic knowledge?	Number (N = 86)	Percentage
Yes	72	83.72
No	14	16.28

Table 5. Comparison of before and after coming to Malaysia in the understanding of Islam.

Q: Compared to while you were in China, how would you describe your understanding of Islam after coming to Malaysia?	Number (N = 79)	Percentage
My understanding of Islam has become more moderate	59	74.68
My understanding of Islam has become more conservative	2	2.53
My understanding of Islam has not changed	18	22.78

Table 6. Benefits to be derived from studying in Malaysia (multi-selection permitted).

Q: What are the major benefits to be derived from studying and living in Malaysia?	Number (N = 88)
Increase in Islamic knowledge and strengthening of one's faith	70
Learning of professional skill and knowledge	45
Expansion of one's horizon	73
Improvement in English	63

affirmatively to become Malaysian citizen, while 34 respondents preferred to go back to China, and the remaining 16 answered 'unsure'. Within this question also, we provided space for respondents to explain their reasons. Among those who answered affirmatively, many cited the fact that this is a Muslim country, showing that religious identity was in fact important in making their choice over citizenship. While for those who preferred to go back to China, among the reasons were the pride of being a Chinese citizen and patriotism (Table 8).

Theoretical discussion

Constrained by the domestic laws and policies in China governed by the officially atheistic communist party, what would happen to the identity among the Chinese Muslim community in Malaysia, who are residing in a Muslim-majority country (though not a pluralist democracy) where outward expression of religious (Islamic) identity is not only permitted but encouraged? The above findings suggest that identities of the Chinese Muslims were subjected to two forms of encountering with the 'others' that have the effects of not diluting but strengthening the Chinese Muslim identity. There was no question that many of them found the strengthening of their Islamic faith in Malaysia, but at the same time, many also sensed their differences from other Muslims (Malays). Henceforth, while within China they might

Table 7. Overseas Chinese Muslims' attitudes towards Malaysia and China.

According to your experience in Malaysia and China, please indicate your agreement or disagreement over the following statements	Strongly disagree	Disagree	Hard to say	Agree	Strongly agree	Total (N =)
Malaysia is a democratic country	0 (0.0per cent)	10 (13.15)	30 (39.47)	33 (43.42)	3 (3.94)	76
Malaysia is an Islamic state	0 (0.0)	6 (7.79)	16 (20.77)	43 (55.84)	12 (15.78)	77
Malaysia is a secular state, but with Muslims as the majority of the population	0 (0.0)	8 (10.96)	20 (27.40)	37 (50.68)	8 (10.96)	73
Laws in Malaysia should have more Islamic elements	1 (1.33)	4 (5.33)	22 (29.33)	44 (58.67)	4 (5.33)	75
There is a trend towards Islamization in Malaysia	1 (1.35)	8 (10.81)	34 (45.95)	30 (40.54)	1 (1.35)	74
Malaysia's policy towards Muslims from China is good	1 (1.56)	13 (20.00)	26 (40.00)	29 (45.31)	5 (7.81)	64
Malaysia's human rights record is good	1 (1.33)	5 (6.67)	35 (46.67)	34 (45.33)	0 (0.0)	75
China is a democratic country	11 (14.86)	22 (29.73)	25 (33.78)	16 (21.62)	0 (0.0)	74
Although China adopts a socialist system, it respects people's freedom of religion	10 (13.51)	21 (28.37)	25 (33.78)	17 (22.97)	1 (1.35)	74
The development of Islam in China is well	7 (9.46)	24 (32.43)	25 (33.78)	18 (24.32)	0 (0.0)	74
Islam in China should have characteristics of its own	5 (6.76)	8 (10.81)	24 (32.43)	31 (41.89)	6 (8.11)	74
China's policy towards ethnic minorities is satisfactory	10 (14.08)	21 (29.57)	27 (38.03)	12 (16.90)	1 (1.41)	71
China's sovereign territorial claims are legitimate	2 (2.82)	5 (7.04)	33 (46.48)	24 (33.80)	7 (9.86)	71
All Muslim nationalities of China belong to the *Zhonghua Minzu* (the Chinese Nation)	1 (1.35)	3 (4.05)	11 (14.86)	40 (54.05)	19 (24.66)	74
Chinese Muslims in overseas should contribute to the promotion of Chinese culture	0 (0.0)	1 (1.37)	12 (16.44)	37 (50.68)	23 (31.51)	73
Chinese Muslims in Malaysia help to contribute to the political, economic, and cultural development of China and Malaysia	1 (1.37)	2 (2.73)	17 (23.29)	38 (52.05)	15 (20.55)	73

Table 8. Malaysian Citizenship vs. Chinese Citizenship.

Q: If conditions permitted, would you like to become Malaysia's citizens	Number ($N = 78$)	Percentage
Yes	27	34.61
No	34	43.58
Unsure	17	21.79

want to emphasize more their Muslim faith to differentiate from the non-Muslim Chinese, outside of China, they may want to emphasize more their Chinese heritage to differentiate themselves from the non-Chinese Muslims. This can be clearly seen in the elite interviews, where all elites/civic leaders of the Chinese Muslim community expressed strongly that the Chinese cultural heritage must be passed on to the future generations. However, on the other hand, as can be seen in the activities of OCMA in cultivating relationship in helping with the disaster relief work in Malaysia and cultivating ties with the Malaysian officialdom, there is also the continued emphasis on 'Muslim connections' between the Chinese Muslims and Malay Muslims, sometimes for the facilitation of business ties.

On the other hand, the encounter with the non-Muslim Malaysian Chinese reinforced their sense of being a minority group of China, as they compare themselves with the Malaysian Chinese as a 'successful' ethnic minority. As shown in the elite interview data above, many overseas Chinese Muslim elites interpret the 'success' of this ethnic minority in Malaysia as at least partly due to the Chinese culture, and the struggle of the ethnic Chinese in Malaysia to preserve this culture although under governmental pressure. The encountering with this form of minority 'success' appeals to the Chinese Muslims because they share the linguistic, ethnic and cultural ties with the ethnic Chinese in Malaysia and in this sense, it is reinforcing their ethnic and cultural identity as Chinese. In Laitin's rational choice language, the presence of Malaysian Chinese reinforced the state of equilibrium of their identity as Chinese Muslims and there is so far very little incentive to 'tip' or 'cascade' towards a new form of identity (Laitin 1998). In our interactions with the elite leaders, the theme that overseas Chinese Muslims and the Malaysian Chinese are the same as ethnic Chinese (*doushi huaren*) was always present. As can be seen by the elite interview, by emphasizing the 'ethnic Chinese' label, they also foster cultural ties and linkages with the local Chinese community and this can also be advantageous to their cultural and business agenda. In short, in encountering with the two different ethnic groups in Malaysia, the Malay-Muslims and ethnic Chinese, and in the multi-ethnic context of Malaysia, the overseas Chinese Muslims so far found that their dual identity can be strategically advantageous to them.

The category of 'Chinese' (huaren), however, is extremely flexible as well. While in Malaysia these overseas Chinese Muslims see 'Chinese' as an ethnic category, back to China, the category of 'Chinese' reverts to become a national identity category and Hui (or other ethnicity) becomes their primary ethnic categorization as a minority. This can be observed in their relationship with the Han Chinese from China and the official China. While ethnic pride with the Han Chinese is mostly accepted and praised upon when the Han Chinese are the Malaysian Chinese, not the Han Chinese from China –the actual majority in their own country. In the latter case, there has been much less active cultivation of ties and interaction. In other words, the 'familiar stranger' description of the relationship between the Han and the Hui within China is played out in overseas as well. That the same kind of ethnic relations is played out in a different context can be seen in the case of Uyghur–Hui ties as well. In China, the relationship between these two Muslim ethnic groups is generally tense although they share the same religion. In the Muslim-majority Malaysia, there is no sign that both groups have better interactions. Through-out our research, we have not been able to make meaningful connection with the overseas Uyghur Muslims despite their (assumed) sizable presence in Malaysia.

Finally, the factor of the state cannot be discounted. As discussed in the activities of OCMA, and revealed in the elite interviews and the survey of Chinese Muslim students (especially Table 7 above), the Chinese Muslims are much aware of (and critical of) the restrictive policies of the Chinese state, and have been careful about interacting with the official Chinese side (symbolized by the Chinese Embassy); yet, ironically, they also in general accept the official Chinese discourse of *Zhonghua minzu* (Chinese Nation) and that the Chinese Muslims are part of this great nation. Being proud of their Chinese heritage at the same time, many of these overseas Chinese Muslims also display critical attitudes towards the Chinese government and mainstream society. In other words, increased exposure to the wider Islamic world, and freer expression of their religious identity in a different political context, has not necessarily led to dilution of the Chinese ethnic and national identity and the emergence of a new kind of national consciousness, as suggested by Danforth above. A qualification has to be made here in the sense that the restrictive immigration policies of the Malaysian government in effect preclude the possibility of many of these Chinese Muslims to become Malaysian citizens, and hence in a way make their choice to remain as a Chinese national easier. Despite this being the case, and having coming from a socialist state, many Chinese Muslims maintain a positive view of Malaysia because of its permissiveness towards religion and Islam in particular, and tend not to focus too much on the tension between the secular and Islamic tendencies in the country.

In following up Gladney's discussion of how connection with the wider Islamic world impacts upon the relationship between Chinese Muslims and China, so far, the evidence presented in this paper is that despite this exposure, there are many Chinese Muslims who remain proud of their Chinese national, ethnic and cultural identity. The research here partially confirms those scholars who express scepticism towards the incompatibility thesis between Islam and the Chinese order.

Conclusion

In the Muslim-majority countries that have friendly ties with China, increasingly, there have been more and more Muslim students, businesspersons, academics and professionals from China staying and working in these countries. Increasingly, the new Chinese Muslim community that is being formed in Malaysia and examined in this paper is similarly emerging in other countries such as United Arab Emirates, Indonesia, Egypt, Turkey and others. As mentioned before, this group of Chinese Muslims is different from the traditional, mostly Han Chinese diaspora, and also not the same with the separatist Uyghur groups. This phenomenon is likely to become more common as China expands its influences in and connections with the Muslim countries, and yet it has not been widely studied in the academic world. Studies of this kind of transnational community and network therefore can draw interesting theoretical implications. It is hoped that this paper has made a modest contribution to the literature in its attempt to shed some lights of the new overseas Chinese Muslim community emerging in Malaysia.

Through introducing the history of the formation of such community in Malaysia, the activities of the main organization representing this community, elite interviews, and the supplementary data from a survey of the Chinese Muslim students in Malaysia, this research shows that while Islam certainly appeals to Chinese Muslims and for many of them it remains their most important identity, it does not necessarily lead to a renouncement of their Chinese heritage. The presence of a sizable ethnic Chinese minority in Malaysia reinforces their cultural Chinese identification. Nevertheless, this study is preliminary in nature, with more field research necessary, and comparative studies of similar communities in other countries will yield greater insights about the question of identity. For instance, in other Muslim-majority countries where there is only a negligible presence of ethnic Chinese (Han or otherwise), how might that affect the identity of transnational Chinese Muslim group? Another possibility is the virtual (online) transnational networking aspect of the community, which this paper briefly touches upon but has not dealt with in depth.

Note

1. According to Liang (2012), there are roughly 190,000 (disputed number, though) Hui people outside of China.

Acknowledgements

The authors would like to acknowledge the assistance provided by Overseas Chinese Muslim Association (OCMA) and Regional Islamic Da'wah Council of Southeast Asia and the Pacific (RISEAP) in the course of the research of this paper.

Disclosure statement

No potential conflict of interest was reported by the authors.

Funding

The research is partially supported by [UMRG RP025–15HNE].

References

Allès, E. 2005. "The Chinese-Speaking Muslims (Dungans) of Central Asia: A Case of Multiple Identities in A Changing Context." *Asian Ethnicity* 6 (2): 121–134.

Barabantseva, E.. 2012. Who are 'Overseas Chinese Ethnic Minorities'? China's Search for Transnational Ethnic Unity." *Modern China* 38 (1): 78–109.

Bryman, A. 2012. *Social Research Methods*. 4th ed. New York, NY: Oxford University Press.

Chen, X. 2015. "Chinese Muslims in Canada: A Demographic Profile and A Preliminary Test of Ethnic Saliency." *Asian Ethnicity* 16 (4): 538–548.

Danforth, L. M. 1995. *The Macedonian Conflict: Ethnic Nationalism in A Transnational World*. Princeton, NJ: Princeton University Press.

Dexter, L. A. 1970. *Elite and Specializing Interviewing*. Evanston, IL: Northwestern University Press.

Gladney, D. C. 1996. *Muslim Chinese: Ethnic Nationalism in the People's Republic*. Cambridge, MA: Harvard University Press.

Gladney, D. C. 2003. "'Islam in China: Accommodation or Separatism?" *China Quarterly* 174: 451–467.

Hew, W. W. 2014. "Beyond "Chinese Diaspora" and "Islamic Ummah": Various Transnational Connections and Local Negotiations of Chinese Muslim Identities in Indonesia." *SOJOURN: Journal of Social Issues in Southeast Asia* 29 (3): 627–656.

Ho, W. Y. 2013. "Mobilizing the Muslim Minority for China's Development: Hui Muslims, Ethnic Relations and Sino-Arab Connections." *Journal of Comparative Asian Development* 12 (1): 84–112.

Isaacs, H. R. 1975. *Idols of the Tribe: Group Identity and Political Change*. Cambridge, MA: Harvard University Press.

Laitin, D. D. 1998. *Identity in Formation: The Russian-Speaking Populations in the Near Abroad*. Ithaca, NY: Cornell University Press.

Liang, L. L. 2012. "Ningxia Huizu huaqiao huaren shehui yu xianzhuang chutan." [A preliminary exploration of the Ningxia Hui overseas Chinese society and present situation.] *Huizu yanjiu* [Studies of Hui Nationality] 2: 109–116.

Lipman, J. N. 2004. "White Hats, Oil Cakes, and Common Blood: The Hui in the Contemporary Chinese State." In *Governing China's Multiethnic Frontiers*, edited by M. Rossabi, 19–52. Seattle, WA: University of Washing Press.

Ma, R. W. 2005a. "The Hui Diaspora." In *Encyclopedia of Diasporas*, edited by M. Ember, C. Ember, and I. Skoggerd, 113–124. Berlin: Springer.

Ma, R. W. 2005b. "Shifting Identities: Chinese Muslims in Malaysia." *Asian Ethnicity* 6 (2): 89–107.

Ma, Y. F., and Z. B. Yang. 1988. *Aiziha'er daxue* [Al Azhar University]. Changsha: Hunan jiaoyu chubanshe.

Muzakki, A. 2010. "Ethnic Chinese Muslims in Indonesia: An Unfinished Anti-Discrimination Project." *Journal of Muslim Minority Affairs* 30 (1): 81–96.

RISEAP. 1982. "Tunku Leads Delegation to Visit Muslims in China." *Al-Nahdah: A Quarterly Journal of the Regional Islamic Da'wah Council of Southeast Asia and the Pacific* 2 (1): 42.

RISEAP. 1988. "RISEAP's Officials Meet Muslim Leaders in China." *Al-Nahdah: A Quarterly Journal of the Regional Islamic Da'wah Council of Southeast Asia and the Pacific* 8 (3–4): 64.

RISEAP. 1995. "RISEAP Delegation Visits China." *Al-Nahdah: A Quarterly Journal of the Regional Islamic Da'wah Council of Southeast Asia and the Pacific* 15 (3–4): 36–37.

Robinson, F. 1994. "Islam and Nationalism." In *Nationalism*, edited by J. Hutchinson, and A. D. Smith, 214–217. New York, NY: Oxford University Press.

Vasantkumar, C. 2012. "What is This "Chinese" in Overseas Chinese? Sojourn Work and the Place of China's Minority Nationalities in Extraterritorial Chinese-Ness." *Journal of Asian Studies* 71 (2): 423–446.

Vertovec, S. 2001. "Transnationalism and Identity." *Journal of Ethnic and Migration Studies* 27 (4): 573–582.

Wong, D. (trans. ZHANG H. P.) 2013. "Musilin de liudong yu Zhongguo xinyimin: Malaixiya Huizu liudong ge'an yanjiu." [Muslim mobility and new Chinese migration: A case study of Hui mobility in Malaysia.] *Huaqiao Huaren lishi yanjiu [Studies of Overseas Chinese History]* 2: 13–27.

Xie, Y. J., X. H. Shu, and M. L. Ma. 2002. *Yisilan sixiang yu Huizu shehui de xietiao fazhan* [Islamic Thought and its Coordinated Development with Hui Society]. Yinchuan: Ningxia renmin chubanshe.

Yao, J. D. 1999. "Zhongguo liu'Ai Huizu xuesheng paiqian shimo." [The Beginning and End of China's Hui Students in Egypt.] *Huizu yanjiu [Studies of Hui Nationality]* 1: 59–63.

Zhao, H. M. 2004. *Shaoshu minzu huaqiao huaren yanjiu* [Studies of Overseas Chinese Ethnic Minorities]. Beijing: Zhongguo huaqiao chubanshe.

Zhao, D. 2014. "Religious Identity and Cultural Refashioning: Educational Constraints for Migrant Muslim Hui University Students in China." *Diaspora, Indigenous, and Minority Education* 8 (2): 59–74.

Kazakh perspective on China, the Chinese, and Chinese migration

Aziz Burkhanov[a] and Yu-Wen Chen[b,c]

[a]Graduate School of Public Policy, Nazarbayev University, Astana, Kazakhstan; [b]Department of World Cultures, University of Helsinki, Helsinki, Finland; [c]Department of Asian Studies, Palacky University, Olomouc, Czech Republic

ABSTRACT

Discourse analysis of different languages of newspapers in Kazakhstan reveals that Kazakhstanis' views towards China and the Chinese are divided. The official discourse in both state-sponsored Russian and Kazakh newspapers is in accordance with the country's policy towards further engagement with their rising Chinese neighbour. However, negative stereotypes of China and the Chinese, as well as sinophobia, are pervasive in private Kazakh language newspapers. Private Russian newspapers have a more nuanced view towards China, with a hidden inclination towards being critical of that country and its people. Although the majority of these societal voices do not have a direct impact on changing the national policies of Kazakhstan, they are important in the sense that Kazakhstan's ruling elite must continue to gauge social views and to placate differences in order to secure the stability and legitimacy of the regime.

Introduction

Since the new post-Soviet states emerged in Central Asia in 1991, China has been seeking to foster diplomatic, political, and economic relations with these new territories (Clarke 2011; Schoen and Kaylan 2014). The official lines of Central Asian states are also moving towards benign relations with their growing Chinese neighbour. However, Laruelle and Peyrouse (2012) noted that the Central Asian populace does not look on Beijing's inroads into the region as favourably as do official discourses from Central Asian governments. The crux of this analysis lies in delving into this local perspective. The country under investigation is Kazakhstan, which is a good starting point for examination because it is geographically close to China. As the country is normally considered a leading player in Central Asia, an assessment of how its populace perceives China and the Chinese would provide an indication of how other Central Asians respond to their rising powerful neighbour.

Another factor that makes Kazakhstan an interesting case for analysis is that the country is ethnically diverse. It is undergoing the process of nation-building, with significant ethnic minorities having presence in Kazakhstan, and two languages, that is, Kazakh and Russian, being widely used in the media and everyday life (Burkhanov and Sharipova 2014; Spehr and Kassenova 2012). In a similar manner to other Central Asian countries, Kazakhstani society is seeking a way to define its national identity. It is a daunting task, as the Kazakh national patriots and Russian nationalist groups have apparently different interests in this nation-building process (Bremmer 1994; Brubaker 2011; Yemelianova 2014; Zardykhan 2004). The stability of the country and the legitimacy of the ruling elite will ultimately be affected by whether the regime can find a way to appeal to these two strikingly different groups. The aim of our analysis was to understand different views and narratives that exist in the country with regard to an increasingly salient 'other', that is, the rising Chinese neighbour, as well as the Chinese in Kazakhstani society.

There follows an overview of Kazakhstan's increasing ties with China, and then our conceptual basis which borrows from various international findings on how the media serves as a source of public debate in general and in Kazakhstan specifically. In the methodology section, we explain how we selected and used discourse analysis to examine the stances of different newspapers (public vs. private; Russian vs. Kazakh) with regard to their Chinese neighbour and the Chinese inside Kazakhstan. The second last part of this paper presents the empirical findings and our conclusions are drawn in the final section.

Sino–Kazakhstani relations

At the state level, both Beijing and Astana believe that fostering relations is beneficial. Economically, China needs Kazakhstan to supply the raw materials and natural resources (e.g. hydrocarbons, oil, gas, minerals) that it requires for its own development, while, in turn, Kazakhstan needs basic consumer goods and finished products from China (O'Neill 2014; Shambaugh and Yahuda 2008). In the domain of regional security, both China and Central Asia are aware of the advantages of cooperation to strengthen their borders and to prevent any separatist or extremist movements (e.g. those originating from the Uyghurs) from developing and multiplying (Chen 2014).

As a result of China's interest in Central Asia, Beijing has developed a Central Asia policy with emphasis on peace, cooperation and development. From the more security-oriented Shanghai Cooperation Organization to the most recent Silk Road Economic Belt initiative, China stresses that there is equality among participating countries and the cooperative efforts are supposed to result in mutual benefits.[1] China does not want its efforts to be interpreted as the creation of a new great game nor its ambition to generate new sphere of influence in Central Asia.

Despite China's disclaimer of its ambitions in Central Asia, most observers do see the rising competition of great powers in the region (Clarke 2008; Ziegler and Rajan 2014). This is in line with numerous discussions, in academia as well as in public debate, regarding whether the ascent of China poses threats or could bring peace to world politics (Aldrich, Lu, and Liu 2014; Chu, Liu, and Huang 2014; Liu and Chu 2014; Mearsheimer 2010). Different countries have reacted to this challenge in a variety of ways. Some have contended that East Asian and Southeast Asian countries are neither balancing nor bandwagoning against China (Cheng and Hsu 2005; Kang 2009; Kuik 2008). Rather, they have tried to keep all strategic options open, allowing the possibility of including both elements of balancing and bandwagoning in coping with their relations with that country. This is exemplified in the way Kazakhstan addresses relations with China as well.

More specifically, Kazakhstan has a so-called 'multi-vector' foreign policy that is not only aimed at tackling the challenge of the rise of China, but also at helping Kazakhstan cope with the ever-challenging international environment on various fronts. Kazakhstan is a massive country in terms of size, but a relatively small power when it comes to other indicators, such as economic power and political clout. Due to geographic vicinity, the presence of large Kazakh minority in China's Xinjiang as well as the large Uyghur population in Kazakhstan, China has always had a place in Kazakhstan's foreign policy (Clarke 2014).

Kazakhstan, however, is not only close to China. It is also near Russia and has traditionally been influenced by Russia. Neighbouring two giants makes the ruling elite aware of the necessity of striking a balanced relationship with its giant neighbours, while still maintaining its own sovereignty. The multi-vector foreign policy serves this purpose, as well as helping to signal to countries around the world that Kazakhstan is on good terms with many nations, raising its stance and image in world politics (Chen 2015).

In addition to serving Kazakhstan's external interests, the multi-vector foreign policy has the merit of speaking to domestic constituents (Burkhanov and Sharipova 2014; Clarke 2014), which is clearly exhibited in Kazakhstan's relationship with China (Clarke 2014). In order to help maintain its legitimacy in governing the country,[2] the ruling elite have used the multi-vector policy to avoid blame and to take credit. When the public is supportive of a certain government undertaking with China, the government triumphantly proclaims this as an achievement of its multi-vector policy with regard to establishing a good relationship with Beijing. Conversely, when society is not satisfied with the government's handling of certain issues with China, such as the 2008–2009 controversy over Kazakhstan's lease of a massive swathe of land to that neighbour, the government avoided blame by arguing that it never attempted to favour any other countries at the cost of Kazakhstan's interests (Chen 2015).

A review of the current literature shows that Central Asians, including those in Kazakhstan, generally do not necessarily see eye-to-eye with their leaders' gradual prioritization of improving relations with China (Laruelle and Peyrouse 2012). Survey analysis and some expert observations have indicated the existence of phobias and myths when it comes to Kazakhstani citizens' perceptions of China and the Chinese people. For example, there are fears regarding the growing Chinese migration to Kazakhstan, and the wage gap between Chinese and local labourers in the industries of local infrastructure arouse great resentment. The Chinese are viewed as taking away locals' jobs. The influx of Chinese goods into Kazakhstan is also perceived as a threat to local products. Part of this antagonism is supported by facts (Sadovskaya 2007; Syroezhkin 2009). However, Syroezhkin (2009, 2014) cautioned that some of the problems have been dramatized and exaggerated. The lack of accurate and sober understanding of China and Sino–Kazakhstani relations breeds stereotypes, sinophobia, and myths. Even at the expert level, there is a paucity of researchers who are studying contemporary China and who are capable of offering impartial views on that country and its people, as well as an absence of expert views on the specificities of Sino–Kazakhstani relations (Clarke 2014; Syroezhkin 2009, 2014).

Although they are few in number, some studies have revealed a regional difference in local perceptions. For example, the residents of Almaty, which is the old political and administrative capital of Kazakhstan, and which has a longer history of exchanges with China, show a greater knowledge of that country than do residents in other parts of the country (Syroezhkin 2009). In Central and Western regions of Kazakhstan, awareness of Chinese culture, history, and traditions is the lowest, compared to other areas of the country (Sadovskaya 2007; Syroezhkin 2009). It has also been found that the public is more interested in economic development, foreign policy, and socio-demographic issues in China than in Chinese culture. This reflects the fact that issues that concern citizens in Kazakhstan are more practically oriented (Syroezhkin 2009).

We delved into this perceptual difference by discerning the views stated in Russian and Kazakh newspapers. These newspapers have different target audiences, and represent the views of different ethnic groups in the country. As noted previously, the ruling elite in Kazakhstan has an interest in consolidating its ruling legitimacy. On one level, they must find a way to satisfy and balance the needs of the ethnic Russians and Kazakh nationalists whose divergent views could tear the country apart. Addition of the China factor complicates the task, because the regime's growing ties with China, for apparently important national interests, are not necessarily well-received at the public level. We employed discourse analysis of newspapers of different languages to reveal the narratives that different sectors of Kazakh society have been weaving, accepting, and debating, with regard to China and the Chinese people. In the next section, we clarify why we used the media, that is, the newspapers, to gauge perceptual differences in Kazakhstan.

Media as sources of discourses

Since Kazakhstan gained independence, its number of media outlets has grown dramatically. In the late 1980s, the total number of registered media outlets was only 10 republic-level printed media and 21 TV and radio channels. In 2012, the total number of registered media outlets at all levels was 2765, including 1619 newspapers and 848 magazines (MediaLaw Internews Project 2010; Ministry of Culture and Information Statistics 2012). The state vs. non-state media ownership breakdown demonstrates that the state remains not only a regulator, but also a significant player in the media market. Of the 2765 registered media outlets in 2012, 439 (16%) were owned by the state and 2326 (84%) were privately owned. Printed media accounted for over 90% of the total number of registered media outlets, including the 1619 newspapers, among which 328 (20%) are owned by the state, and 1291 (80%) are privately owned. Of the 848 magazines, 636 (79%) are privately owned and 172 (21%) are state-owned. Language breakdown statistics show that in May 2013, 344 media outlets operated in only Kazakh, 758 in only Russian, 727 in both Kazakh and Russian, and 282 in Kazakh, Russian, and other languages. Approximately 33 printed media outlets were published in 15 different languages of various ethnic groups of Kazakhstan. However, these numbers do not necessarily mean that all of these media outlets actually operate actively in the market – in certain cases they are technically registered, but have been put in a 'sleeping mode' to be activated and used in the future; in addition, this number includes a significant number of papers that have been created only to print private advertisements. However, despite the massive privatization campaign of the media outlets in the early 1990s, and the fact that, unlike in the Soviet era, newspapers can benefit from advertisements, sales, and subscription incomes in the post-independence period, most newspapers in Kazakhstan are not profitable or financially self-sufficient. Rather, they depend on patron state agencies or private owners to finance their operations (Junisbai 2011).

The media in Kazakhstan has a lot in common with the Soviet press–where the media were not expected to inform the audience about current events, but instead, were used to transmit ideological messages from the Communist party. Another important similarity is the lack of connection with the market imperatives. In the Soviet Union, newspapers had guaranteed funding from the State and never had to worry about profits or finances – something we see replicating in today's Kazakhstan. Most media outlets are not profitable and depend on their sponsors and parent companies on funding.[3]

As various studies have shown (Maxwell and Shaw 1972; Wanta, Golan, and Lee 2004), the media in general in various parts of the world have the capability to 'set the agenda' for domestic and international politics. They not only inform the audience of politically salient issues, but also influence readers' evaluations of these issues by interpreting news in a positive or negative fashion. In ethnically diverse and multilingual societies, the media can also reflect different perceptions, prejudices, and stereotypes that various ethnic groups possess or express about one another, as well as about neighbouring countries, and thus contribute to the perception of these nations that is held by mass audiences. It is with this in mind that we decided to use discourse analysis to study newspapers in Kazakhstan.

Newspapers studied and their readers

Four of Kazakhstan's nationwide print newspapers with the largest circulation size were chosen for examination: *Egemen Qazaqstan* [*Independent Kazakhstan*] and *Zhas Alash* [*Young Alash*] printed in Kazakh, and *Kazakhstanskaia Pravda* [*Truth of Kazakhstan*] and *Vremia* [*Time*] published in Russian. *Kazakhstanskaia Pravda* and *Egemen Qazaqstan* are two major government-owned nationwide newspapers that are used to express the regime's officially sanctioned view on major political and social issues in Kazakhstan. They were both founded in the early 1920s, and for a long time were the official organs of the Communist Party of the Kazakh Soviet Socialist Republic. In independent Kazakhstan, they have continued the decades-long Soviet tradition of the pro-government newspapers; however, after the collapse of the Soviet Union, they did adjust their practices in order to appear more like genuine newspapers and not just propaganda organs of the Communist Party. Their audiences consist primarily of public servants working at government agencies, regional and municipal administrations, and the so-called *biudzhetniki*; employees of state-funded institutions, such as public hospitals and high schools. In 2011, circulation of *Kazakhstanskaia Pravda* was estimated at approximately 100,000 copies, with a corresponding figure of 170,000 copies for *Egemen Qazaqstan*.

The Russian-language official paper tends to represent direct governmental views. Relatively speaking, the Kazakh-language official paper can maintain more critical distance and take more critical positions vis-à-vis the government policies than the Russian-language official paper.

The Russian-language *Vremia* and the Kazakh-language *Zhas Alash* represent another segment of the newspaper market of Kazakhstan. These newspapers are technically privately owned (although *Vremia* is technically owned by an industrial group indirectly affiliated with the government) and, as such, are far less limited by governmental discourse. They often take contrasting positions in their coverage of political and social issues, compared with *Kazakhstanskaia Pravda* and *Egemen Qazaqstan*. *Zhas Alash*, known as *Lenin-shil Zhas* [*Leninist Youth*] in the Soviet era, is sympathetic towards the Kazakh-speaking intelligentsia in its editorial policies, including those intellectuals with rather nationalist views; its circulation size is estimated at approximately 50,000 copies. *Vremia* inherited most of the journalists and concepts from *Karavan*, a famous and extremely popular newspaper of the 1990s. After *Karavan* expressed harsh criticism of the regime, owner Boris Gillner was forced to sell the newspaper and emigrate; the entire journalist staff left the paper in protest and started *Vremia*. Although it is under the patronage of the state-owned corporation, Kazakhmys, the paper has managed to preserve its quasi-independent editorial policies. Its circulation is approximately 180,000 for the weekly edition, and around 30,000 for the daily edition, making it by far the most popular private newspaper in the country.

Kazakhstan has a complicated language situation, which has political, social, economic, and cultural implications, and which also affects newspaper readership. The language issue is one of the most sensitive factors in domestic policy in post-independence Kazakhstan. Russian gradually became the dominant language in Kazakhstan over the course of the Soviet era, due to a massive campaign of Russification. Schools and universities adopted Russian as the language of instruction, and, although the Russian-language schools of Kazakhstan offered Kazakh language lessons, most students did not take this requirement seriously. Pupils usually graduated from schools with no, or very minimal, knowledge of Kazakh, and felt no need to improve it. In contrast, as Russian was necessary to secure a successful career in Soviet society, most urban Kazakhs learned in Russian schools, kindergartens, and universities and came to use Russian as their principal means of communication. Kazakh was granted state language status only by Language Law 24 of 1989, which was an important symbolic marker, although limited efforts were made in terms of its implementation (Fierman 1998).

After independence, the 1993 Constitution of Kazakhstan confirmed the status of Kazakh as the state language and Russian as a language of interethnic communication. However, in 1995, the new Constitution amended this situation and, while continuing to grant Kazakh the status of the only state language, it also allowed Russian to be used officially on an equal basis in state agencies. In practice, implementation of stricter Kazakh language policies, although officially declared, has faced a number of problems, mainly due to lack of resources and inefficient policies. Measures aimed at enhancing usage of the Kazakh language have frequently been used as a justification for silencing oppositional media, mainly printed in Russian. In other cases, the media only formally comply with the legal requirements by broadcasting in Kazakh late at night and filling the Kazakh-language segment with low quality music video clips and movies from the Soviet era. Fluency in the Kazakh language remains limited among Russians and other ethnic groups of Kazakhstan. As some observers have argued (Bremmer 1994; Burkhanov and Sharipova 2014; Zardykhan 2004), for the Russians, it is probably a psychological factor that is the most significant barrier with regard to studying the Kazakh language. During the Soviet era, most Russians perceived Russian as being superior to Kazakh and now find themselves in the reverse situation; having to learn the language they have long considered as being inferior. They perceive the state promotion of the Kazakh language as unfair towards Russian and Russian-speakers, and some have appealed for Russian to be granted the status of the second state language. In contrast, Kazakh nationalist groups continue to criticize the government for not being sufficiently persistent in making Kazakh the genuine *de facto* state language, and view this as another manifestation of a colonial mentality and disrespect for Kazakh culture and language (Bremmer 1994; Burkhanov and Sharipova 2014; Zardykhan 2004).

The language distribution logically affects the audiences of the newspapers studied. As many observers have pointed out (Bremmer 1994; Brubaker 2011; Burkhanov and Sharipova 2014; Zardykhan 2004), the linguistic composition divides modern Kazakhstan society into two major groups with two distinctly different visions regarding the path that Kazakhstan should take to build its country. The first group includes so-called 'cosmopolitans', the urbanized and predominantly Russian-speaking population, who constitute the majority of the *Kazakhstanskaia Pravda* and *Vremia* audiences; the second group is the Kazakh-speaking 'ethnonationalists', who prefer to read *Egemen Qazaqstan* and *Zhas Alash*. As Surucu (2005) asserted, this division cuts sharply across ethnic boundaries and extrapolates further to the attitude towards modernization and vision of the state, with the ultimate question of what kind of modernization path Kazakhstan should follow. The 'cosmopolitans' deny Kazakh traditionalism, as they consider it backward and 'un-modern', and tend to orient to the examples of Western countries or Russia. Most of the members of this group have received their education in Russian-language schools and universities, and use Russian as their primary channel of communication; they live primarily in urban areas, such as Almaty, Astana, and *oblast* [regional] centres.

In contrast, Kazakh-speaking 'ethnonationalists', who make up the bulk of the *Egemen Qazaqstan* and *Zhas Alash* audiences, tend to focus on national consolidation and the renaissance of the Kazakhs. From their perspective, modern Kazakhstan is a statehood of ethnic Kazakhs, built on the historical legacy of *khans* [rulers], *batyrs* [warriors], and *biis* [judges] of the historical

Kazakh Khanate and traditional nomadic Kazakh culture. Most of the members of this group are Kazakh-speaking Kazakhs who were educated in Kazakh-language high schools, predominantly in rural areas, and who later migrated to urban areas, seeking better opportunities. The fact that many of these people have left mostly Kazakh-populated rural areas suffering from economic depression, to go to more prosperous and ethnically diverse cities, has led them to develop a sense that Kazakhs are underprivileged in their own country. There is almost no interaction between the two linguistic realms, it happens only rarely; Kazakh-language newspapers follow Russian-language publications and respond to them on their own pages. The Russian discourse practically ignores the Kazakh-language segment, due to the lack of Kazakh proficiency and because readers of Russian-language papers find those in Kazakh uninteresting and as focusing only on praising Kazakh culture and the glorious Kazakh heroes of the past.

Within the scope of this project, we seek to understand how the discourses related to Kazakh and Russian identities circulated in contemporary Kazakhstani society would limit how people in Kazakhstan see the Chinese 'other'. Our approach is inspired by Laclau and Mouffe's (2001) discourse analysis. It is different from critical discourse analysis that would require a more detailed analysis of linguistic practices to allow the exploration of power relationship, and in particular inequalities and power abuses revealed in the studied texts.

The articles selected for analysis in this study were printed in these newspapers between August 2013 and January 2015. They present a variety of genres, including interviews, news reports, reportages, open letters, op-ed columns, editorials, and readers' letters. The Kazakh press especially tends to include more interpretative articles with rather strong opinions rather than just representing news in a neutral tone.

In September 2013, the Chinese leader Xi Jingping visited Kazakhstan and gave a speech at Nazarbayev University, which was founded on the initiative and endorsement of the Kazakhstani president. In that speech, President Xi proposed that China and Central Asia should cooperate in building a Silk Road Economic Belt, leading observers to believe that China's relations with its Central Asian neighbour had reached a culmination. We intend to examine whether this visit by the Chinese president has changed newspapers' discourse on China and the Chinese. It is in this vein that most articles under analysis are between August 2013 (before Xi's visit) and January 2015 (the time we finished writing this paper).

Empirical findings and discussions

We found that the discourses presented in the newspapers studied do not much differ between before and after President Xi's visit to Kazakhstan in September 2013. However, variations do occur between newspapers. As Table 1

Table 1. A typology of public discourse on China in Kazakhstan.

	Russian language newspapers	Kazakh language newspapers
Public (i.e. state-sponsored)	Positive (*Kazakhstanskaia Pravda*)	Positive (*Egemen Qazaqstan*)
Private	Mixed views with inclination towards hidden criticism of China (*Vremia*)	Critical and negative (*Zhas Alash*)

summarizes, state-sponsored newspapers tend to have a positive view of Chinese-Kazakh relations, China, and the Chinese people, while private newspapers show diverse views, with a tendency to be sceptical towards China and the Chinese. Kazakh-language private newspapers exhibit the most hostility towards China. The display of negative and stereotypical images of China and its people is pervasive, demonstrating strong fear and antagonism. The Russian-language private newspaper is often read by conservative businessmen, and, while the discourse regarding China and the Chinese is also somewhat negative, it is frequently less directly expressed.

As politics, economics and the issue of Chinese people in Kazakhstan have been noted by scholars as key areas of discussions in the country (Clarke 2014; Syroezhkin 2009), the following sub-sections present newspaper discussions on these three topics and lead us to identify the way in which China and the Chinese people, as the 'others' are constructed in the media discourse, and therefore in the minds of the citizens of Kazakhstan.

Political cooperation with China

Political cooperation was very frequently discussed in the newspapers, and was mostly described in a neutral-positive tone. With the exception of the Kazakh nationalist *Zhas Alash* newspaper, all other newspapers studied described cooperation projects and exchanges between the leadership of the two countries from a rather positive perspective. As the flagship government-backed newspaper, *Kazakhstanskaia Pravda* offered a particular example of a very positive interpretation of the Kazakhstani–Chinese relationship. The paper emphasized the close personal relationship between the leaders of the two countries as being an important factor in the bilateral relations. For example, in an article entitled 'Leaders of Kazakhstan and China Discussed Cooperation Issues', the newspaper asserted that the leaders of both countries 'very positively' assessed bilateral cooperation dynamics and perspectives (*Kazakhstanskaia Pravda*, September 12, 2014). In an earlier article, the paper reported that the Chinese leader expressed his admiration and support for the Conference on Interaction and Confidence-Building Measures in Asia, the Kazakhstan-backed foreign policy initiative that aims to create an Asian analogue of the Organization for Security and Cooperation in Europe (*Kazakhstanskaia Pravda*, 'China Admires Kazakhstan President's Political Strategic Vision', May 21, 2014). In yet another article, the newspaper reported a meeting between Xi Jinping and Nursultan Nazar-bayev in May 2014, and mentioned that during that meeting several intergo-vernmental agreements, worth eight billion US dollars, were to be signed. The newspaper also praised the fact that the combined worth of all the Chinese economic projects in Kazakhstan, including direct investments, had reached 43 billion US dollars in 2014 (*Kazakhstanskaia Pravda*, 'Nursultan Nazarbayev Will Have Talks with Xi Jinping', May 19, 2014). Similarly, *Egemen Qazaqstan*, the Kazakh-language state-backed paper, reported that China and Kazakhstan will expand cooperation on energy issues, including oil and gas supplies from Western Kazakhstan to China, as well as enhance cooperation on the new energy sources research in connection with the upcoming EXPO-2017 to be held in Astana (*Egemen Qazaqstan*, 'Important Agreement Signed Between Our Country and China', December 6, 2014).

Zhas Alash, the Kazakh-language newspaper that primarily focuses on the Kazakh-speaking Kazakhs' audience, generally experiences less governmental control and frequently adopts a more critical approach towards government policies, including foreign policy. In its discourse on China, *Zhas Alash* often takes fairly prejudiced and negative positions, even when describing political cooperation between the two countries. For example, in 'Chinese Dream Strat-egy of Nur-Otan Party', the paper criticized the government and the leader-ship of Nur-Otan, the ruling political party of Kazakhstan, for too closely replicating Chinese strategic documents and campaigns:

> Chinese leader's strategy called 'Chinese Dream' is similar to our country's strat-egy 'Kazakhstan-2050'. However, we do not want to see Bauyrzhan Baibek [one of the leaders of the Nur-Otan Party] to declare something like this tomorrow: 'from now on we rename our Nur-Otan Party into the Chinese Communist Party Nur-Otan. Our strategies and goals are declared in the Xi Jinping's strategy 'Chinese Dream'.' (*Zhas Alash*, 'Chinese Dream of Nur Otan Party', November 14, 2013)

Zhas Alash also demonstrates and employs general prejudices and suspi-cions towards China, even in contexts that do not directly involve Kazakhstan. In an article called 'Chinese Government Increased the Number of Spies to One Million', the paper described increased security measures in China's law enforcement system, and urged Kazakhstani citizens to use caution when visiting China since the 'street shoe-cleaners, newspaper vendors, parking attendants, ticket counter employees, and hotel concierges' there may all supply information to the Chinese security services, formally or infor-mally (*Zhas Alash*, 'Chinese Government Increased Number of Spies to One Million', June 3, 2014).

Moreover, even fairly neutral and 'safe' government moves and actions often become the target of *Zhas Alash* criticism. In an article dedicated to the new intergovernmental agreement regarding mutual allocation of land in Astana and Beijing for construction of new embassy buildings, either for free or for symbolic lease payments, the newspaper expressed its concerns that a portion of the Kazakh land will be given up to China for 49 years (*Zhas Alash*, 'For Forty-Nine Years ... ', October 30, 2014). In a similar manner, *Zhas Alash* advised the government to allocate more resources to both intelligence and academic research on China and Russia, as well as to create new research centres and think-tanks:

> We think we know China and Russia pretty well. In reality, we know nothing about these countries. If such think-tanks would be working, maybe people from there could talk and fight with the Chinese expansion and Russian imperial ambitions [...] There are many Chinese here now [...] they marry Kazakh wives and pretend becoming Kazakhs. If one [of them] comes here legally, then five come without documents [...]. (*Zhas Alash*, 'Welcoming China Means Giving Up Our Fathers' Tombs', August 16, 2013)

Only in rare instances does *Zhas Alash* take a softer approach towards China and the Kazakhstani–Chinese relationship in general, and, even when it does, it still operates with stereotypical clichés and graphic depictions. For example, in the article 'What Can Kazakhstan Achieve [Sitting] on the Dragon's Tail?', *Zhas Alash* demonstrated a more welcoming approach, stating that, due to all major intergovernmental agreements, Chinese-Kazakhstani relations are developing fairly well and economic cooperation is expanding; therefore, the Kazakhs' traditional fears of China, expressed in a folk proverb, 'Do not step on snake's tail' may no longer be applicable (*Zhas Alash*, 'What Can Kazakhstan Achieve [Sitting] on the Dragon's Tail?', December 23, 2014).

Economic cooperation with China

Economic cooperation was primarily addressed in the state-owned papers, such as *Kazakhstanskaia Pravda* and *Egemen Qazaqstan*, and was also mostly presented in neutral-positive tones. Numerous articles focused on Khorgos, a large commercial and trade hub located at the Kazakhstan-China border, approximately 250 miles east of Almaty. Kazakhstan's leadership pays great attention to this project, and several cooperation initiatives have previously been launched to build a new set of trade facilities at that location. For example, in 'Around Khorgos There May Be a New Town', *Kazakhstanskaia Pravda* described the new Khorgos development project and quoted President Nazarbayev in his expression of hope that 'this long-awaited project, which we implement in cooperation with China, will increase trade between our countries' (*Kazakhstanskaia Pravda*, December 25, 2014).

Kazakhstanskaia Pravda also gave a detailed report of the Kazakhstan-China Business Council meeting, during which several economic agreements, worth 14 billion US dollars, were signed. The Prime Minister of Kazakhstan,

Karim Massimov, stated that the new Kazakhstan governmental strategy 'Nurly Zhol' [Radiate Path] matches well with the 'Silk Road Economic Belt' economic strategy of China, according to the newspaper. Chongqing, an industrial city and a logistical hub in China, appears to particularly benefit from these exchanges because of the new cargo and shipping routes going via Kazakhstan, which will allow for a significant decrease in cargo shipping times between Europe and China (*Kazakhstanskaia Pravda*, 'Bound by One Chain', December 26, 2014). A few days previously, the newspaper reported meetings between Chinese and Kazakh businessmen, in which over 270 Chinese and 230 Kazakh companies participated. Several new agreements were signed, including those between Samruk-Qazyna Holding of Kazakhstan and several major Chinese corporations, including the China General Nuclear Power Corporation, the China International Water and Electric Corporation, the China International Trust and Investment Corporation, and the China National Petroleum Corporation (*Kazakhstanskaia Pravda*, 'Meeting with a Fourteen Billion Effect', December 16, 2014). This was also replicated in the Kazakh-language state-owned newspaper *Egemen Qazaqstan*; its article 'Important Agreement Signed between Our Country and China' focused on the energy cooperation, oil and gas supplies to China, and renewable energy research (*Egemen Qazaqstan*, December 6, 2014).

Interestingly, when narrating these talks, Russian-language *Kazakhstanskaia Pravda* also reported the Kazakhstan government's offer to their Chinese counterparts to move industrial production facilities, such as cement, glass, and agricultural production, to Kazakhstan (*Kazakhstanskaia Pravda*, 'China Moves Industrial Production to Kazakhstan', December 15, 2014; 'PRC Ready to Open Construction and Agricultural Ventures in Kazakhstan', December 15, 2014). This is particularly interesting, as only a few years earlier in 2008–2009, the government of Kazakhstan leaked the fact that it was entering into negotiations with China with regard to leasing some portions of land in Eastern Kazakhstan to that nation for agricultural production, mainly soy, along with bringing thousands of Chinese agricultural workers to Kazakhstan. This led to a very hostile reaction across the political spectrum within Kazakhstan; certainly not expecting this effect, the government has quietly terminated the negotiations. As yet, it remains unclear as to whether many facilities will actually be moved to Kazakhstan, but this idea still appears to benefit from some political support among Kazakhstani government officials. The only major example of this type of economic cooperation briefly mentioned by *Kazakhstanskaia Pravda* was that of the opening of an assembly line in Qostanay, Northern Kazakhstan, by the Chinese car manufacturer Geely. The eventual goal of the venture was to reach a localization level of 50% by 2017 (*Kazakhstanskaia Pravda*, 'Geely Chinese Cars Will Be Assembled in Kazakhstan', October 9, 2014).

Chinese tourists and migrants to Kazakhstan

Cooperation in the tourist industry left the media discourse more divided across linguistic realms, particularly with regard to the issue of Chinese tourists coming to Kazakhstan. Historical stereotypes and prejudices towards the Chinese were manifest in various news reports and commentaries. Russian-language papers followed up on the fact that the Kazakhstan government declared 2017 a year of Chinese tourism in Kazakhstan, with the hope of attracting up to five million Chinese people to visit the EXPO-2017 exhibition in Astana. However, this government initiative was met with criticism and hostility in the Kazakh discourse; the *Zhas Alash* article 'What If Chinese Came … ', which demonstrates existing alarmist stereotypes concerning potential Chinese influx:

> The government wants to attract up to five million Chinese tourists. Why don't they try to attract English or French tourists? […] Of course, since China is way overpopulated, they advise its citizens to go and settle abroad. To let them all in would be a dangerous policy for us since many of them come on fake documents and remain unaccounted. […] China's proposal to adopt visa-free travels for tourists is hence unacceptable for us. It is a way for them to conquer us without a war. (*Zhas Alash*, 'What If Chinese Came', September 9, 2014)

The mutual visa regime between the two countries has existed since Kazakhstan's independence, and the visa application process has been criticized in both countries for long queues at the consulates, poor and uncomfortable waiting facilities, extended processing time for visa applications, complicated bureaucratic procedures, and a long list of documents that are required to be provided in support of visa applications, even for short-term visits. The governments of Kazakhstan and China held several rounds of negotiations around removing, or at least facilitating, the visa regime, beginning with group travels for tourist purposes; however, the very prospect of lifting visa requirements from Chinese citizens when entering Kazakhstan was met with concerns, even in Russian-language papers. The *Vremya* conducted a round of interviews with several prominent policy- and opinion-makers, journalists, and academics, including Murat Auezov, former ambassador of Kazakhstan to China, and the general tone of opinions regarding a lifting of the visa-regime with China ranged from fairly cautious to very negative. For example, Aidos Sarym, a prominent political activist, said:

> Several dozen thousands of Kazakhstani citizens visit China every year, and a million of ethnic Kazakhs live in China and they have to go through the visa application process in order to come here … So, in principle, this [lifting visa requirements] is normal. There is, however, a big danger, that people with bad goals may come without visas claiming to be tourists. (*Vremya*, 'In Waiting Mode [on Visa-Free Regime]', August 10, 2013)

Murat Auezov, former Kazakh ambassador to China, expressed harsh criticism of this initiative, and implied that China has a governmental strategy of encouraging its citizens to go and settle abroad:

China is not a pet dog, it is a tiger! I argue that the visa regime should not only be there, but it should be purposefully very strict […] In China, they regulate their migration – there is a special structure, which tries to put people from one province to one country, so that they could communicate and preserve their loyalty to China and their Chinese identity. (*Vremya*, 'In Waiting Mode [on Visa-Free Regime]', August 10, 2013)

Bulat Abilov, a prominent businessman and former politician, also questioned he government's estimates of the potential number of Chinese tourists travelling to Kazakhstan:

Someone [in the government] mentioned that five million Chinese tourists will visit Kazakhstan [in 2017]. I don't think this estimate is necessarily accurate, since during the entire last year only a few thousand Chinese tourists came. Why would they come here? To see Astana? They have dozens of cities like this, if not hundreds. When talking about visa regime, I think it makes more sense to lift it from citizens of the US and European countries, not necessarily from China. (*Vremya*, 'In Waiting Mode [on Visa-Free Regime]', August 10, 2013)

Furthermore, and related to tourism, the potential illegal migration, and infiltration, of Chinese citizens to Kazakhstan remains a prominent theme in the Kazakh-language papers. General concerns continue to be expressed regarding the potential, and growing, illegal immigration of Chinese citizens to Kazakhstan. These articles and editorial policies frequently express very stereotypical and, at times, even xenophobic, sentiments *vis-à-vis* the Chinese people. For example, in one article, 'How Many Chinese Are Hiding in Kazakhstan?', *Zhas Alash* criticized the government, the law enforcement agencies, and Vice Prime Minister Baqytzhan Sagintayev, personally, for the lack of a coherent and efficient policy for counting and tracking the Chinese visitors once they clear Kazakhstan's border control in airports and bus/train terminals (*Zhas Alash*, May 15, 2014). In another article, 'Mass Migration from China to Kazakhstan Exceeded 19,000 People [in 2014]', *Zhas Alash* reported that, of this number, approximately 13,000 came for 'private visits', around 300 came for 'professional reasons' and also ended up marrying Kazakh women; 244 Chinese citizens moved and settled in Kazakhstan with their entire families. It is unclear from the article whether this number included ethnic Kazakhs who repatriated from China to Kazakhstan or ethnic Chinese (Han) (*Zhas Alash*, 'Mass Migration from China to Kazakhstan Exceeded 19,000 People [in 2014]', November 4, 2014). What is clear is that the narrative towards the Chinese in *Zhas Alash* is negative.

Overall, we found that private newspapers have more coverage of the issue of Chinese citizens in Kazakhstan than public newspapers. Political and economic cooperation with China are mostly covered in public newspapers. This is due to the fact that public newspapers are the mouthpiece of the national policies of which the emphasis is on political and economic cooperation with Beijing. Also, economic cooperation with China is done through deals between huge corporations in both countries. Citizens in small and medium-sized businesses are not directly involved. Hence, citizens are prone to attend to issues with direct impact on their daily life, that is, the implication of Chinese visitors in, and migrants to their country.[4]

If one looks at the divides in Table 1 again, the difference between public and private newspapers actually implies that the private media can to a certain degree express and channel society's reaction to the government's efforts to form a more pro-China discourse as revealed in public newspapers. This echoes the conceptual basis of this paper which stresses the role of the media in reflecting perceptions, prejudices and stereotypes in ethnically diverse societies.

The linguistic divide is more clearly seen between private newspapers of different languages (see Table 1). It is related to a much more important and deep cleavage in the modern Kazakhstani society. To put it simply, the shift from nomadic pastoralism (something that Kazakhs were doing for centuries) to a modern industrial society occurred in a very short time, basically within one generation. This led to a situation where modernity had its roots only in a small fraction of educated urban elite and Russian became associated with the modern path, whereas Kazakh was mostly preserved in the rural areas. Readers of private Kazakh-language and Russian-language newspapers have divergent views on what kind of state Kazakhstan should build and who owns the country. Kazakh-language newspapers tend to emphasize the exclusive 'Kazakhness' of the state; they consider Kazakhs as exclusive legitimate owners of the state since Kazakhstan is the only place where Kazakhs can build a state. In contrast, Russian-language newspapers tend to talk about a 'shared' notion of the state and its poly-ethnic character. It is fair to say that Russian-language newspapers have also developed stereotypical depiction of Kazakh-speaking Kazakhs as coming from remote rural areas, unfamiliar with modern technologies, lacking knowledge about global culture and history, and only concerned with praising glorious Kazakh heroes of the past. Given this context, it is not difficult to understand why China and the Chinese, as the 'others' are not perceived positively in Kazakh newspapers. Relatively speaking, Russian language newspapers can be more inclusive to 'the other' than Kazakh language newspapers as a result. This to some extent speaks to Syroezhkin's (2009) survey result which shows that Kazakhs are more negative towards Chinese migrants than Russians.

Conclusion

In recent years, academic momentum has been gathering with regard to measuring how people around the world view China (Aldrich, Lu, and Liu 2014; Chu, Liu, and Huang 2014; Liu and Chu 2014). Our analysis fills in the void of the Kazakhstani view on the issue, and it reveals that the Kazakhstani views towards China are, in fact, nuanced. The discourse in both state-sponsored Russian and Kazakh newspapers leans towards a positive stance on China, as it is the mouthpiece of national policies that increasingly support engagement with that country. However, in the private sphere, scepticism towards China is evident in Kazakh language newspapers and hidden in Russian language newspapers. Stereotypical images of China and its people, as well as sinophobia, are pervasive in private publications. Although most of these societal voices do not have a direct impact on changing Kazakhstan's national policies, they are important in the sense that the ruling elite must continue to gauge social views and to placate different stances in order to secure the stability and legitimacy of the regime. While this special issue in *Ethnic and Racial Studies* primarily focuses on ethnicities in China, our research contributes to the understanding of how the Chinese as a collectively imagined 'other' are being constructed, and even used for political purposes, in other countries.

Notes

1. See 'Vision and Actions on Jointly Building Silk Road Economic Belt and 21st Century Maritime Silk Road' issued by China's National Development and Reform Commission, Ministry of Foreign Affairs, and Ministry of Commerce on March 2015, http://en.ndrc.gov.cn/newsrelease/201503/t20150330_669367.html (accessed July 19, 2015).
2. The ruling elites of Kazakhstan need legitimacy because of several reasons. To begin with, the ruling elites, led by Nursaltan Nazarbayev did not play a key role in ensuring Kazakhstan's independent statehood. Nazarbayev himself was actually not supportive of the dissolution of the Soviet Union. Hence, the ruling elites lack nationalist legitimacy to run the country. Second, the ruling elites are formed along traditional familial and kinship lines as well as economic and bureaucratic interests. The power is concentrated in the hands of the president, his family, a small group of oligarchs and technocrats. The government, accordingly, has relied on using economic development of the country to boost its legitimacy (i.e. 'performance legitimacy'). The fear for potential Russian irredentism based on the clustering of Russian population in Northern Kazakhstan as well as unresolved territorial disputes with China pose great challenge for the ruling elites to convince its domestic constituents that they are able to maintain Kazakhstan's independent and sovereign statehood. For detailed discussion on the issue of legitimacy, please consult Clarke (2014) and Cummings (2006).
3. The media of the Soviet Union did not exist independently; in most cases, they were placed under the patronage of a Communist Party branch, a government agency, a giant industrial factory or a professional union. The most significant ones were

usually administered under the various republics' Communist Party Central Committee and oblast-level newspapers reported to their respective oblast Party committees. These parent agencies usually provided all necessary funding, technological facilities, managed subscription and distribution channels, and even the cadres; therefore, the newspapers never had to worry about their finances, capital costs or supplies. Even though Soviet newspapers could receive income from advertisements (mostly in the late Soviet era), they almost never depended on the advertisements and subscription incomes in order to survive as they had guaranteed subsidies. In terms of general organizational structure, newspapers and magazines in the Soviet Union were put under strict control of the Communist Party and the security services since their major task was to spread ideological messages from the party and country leadership to the population. In this sense, the newspapers played a different role in Soviet society than in Western countries or even their predecessors in the Russian Empire; the Communist Party viewed their goal as not so much to inform the population about events and news as it was to create and shape interpretations of the events in compliance with Soviet ideology.

4. Issues of Xinjiang and Uyghurs which are supposed to be important in Kazakhstani-Chinese relations but did not appear often in the news article under analysis. Kazakhstani perceptions of Xinjiang is a close and yet distant place. It is close because there are Uyghurs who are culturally, linguistically and religiously connected to Kazakhs. The place is also distant because it is in China. However, despite the fact that Uyghurs are close the Kazakhs, the government of Kazakhstan opts for cooperation with China and had systematically arrested and transferred Uyghur activists to China. Because this is sensitive issue and is highly controlled by the government, it is not covered in the media.

Disclosure statement

No potential conflict of interest was reported by the authors.

References

Aldrich, John, Jie Lu, and Kang Liu. 2014. "How Do Americans View the Rising China?" *Journal of Contemporary China* 24 (92): 203–221.

Bremmer, Ian. 1994. "Nazarbaev and the North: State-Building and Ethnic Relations in Kazakhstan." *Ethnic and Racial Studies* 17 (4): 619–635.

Brubaker, Rogers. 2011. "Nationalizing States Revisited: Projects and Processes of Nationalization in Post-Soviet States." *Ethnic and Racial Studies* 34 (11): 1785–1814.

Burkhanov, Aziz, and Dina Sharipova. 2014. "Kazakhstan's Civic-National Identity: Ambiguous Policies and Points of Resistance." In *Nationalism and Identity Construction in Central Asia: Dimensions, Dynamics, and Directions*, edited by Mariya Y. Omelicheva, 21–36. London: Lexington Books.

Chen, Yu-Wen. 2014. *The Uyghur Lobby: Global Networks, Coalitions and Strategies of the World Uyghur Congress*. London: Routledge.

Chen, Yu-Wen. 2015. "A Research Note on Central Asian Perspectives on the Rise of China: The Example of Kazakhstan." *Issues and Studies* 51 (3): 63–87.

Cheng, Teng-Chi, and Szue-Chin Philip Hsu. 2005. "Between Power Balancing and Bandwagoning: Re-Thinking the Post-Cold War East Asia." In *Rethinking New*

International Order in East Asia: U.S., China, and Taiwan, edited by I. Yuan, 425–460. Taipei: Institute of International Relations and Center for China Studies, National Chengchi University.

Chu, Yun-Han, Kang Liu, and Min-Hua Huang. 2014. "How East Asians View the Rise of China." *Journal of Contemporary China* 24 (93): 398–420.

Clarke, Michael. 2008. "China's Integration of Xinjiang with Central Asia: Securing a Silk Road to Great Power Status?" *China and Eurasia Forum Quarterly* 6 (2): 89–111.

Clarke, Michael. 2011. *Xinjiang and China's Rise in Central Asia – A History.* London: Routledge.

Clarke, Michael. 2014. "Kazakh Responses to the Rise of China: Between Elite Bandwagoning and Societal Ambivalence?" In *Asian Thought on China's Changing International Relations,* edited by Niv Horesh and Emilian Kavalski, 141–172. Basingstoke: Palgrave Macmillan.

Cummings, Sally N. 2006. "Legitimation and Identification in Kazakhstan." *Nationalism and Ethnic Politics* 12: 177–204.

Fierman, William. 1998. "Language and Identity in Kazakhstan: Formulations in Policy Documents 1987–1997." *Communist and Post-Communist Studies* 31 (2): 171–186.

Junisbai, Barbara. 2011. "Oligarchs and Ownership: The Role of Financial-Industrial Groups in Controlling Kazakhstan's 'Independent' Media." In *After the Czars and Commissars: Journalism in Authoritarian Post-Soviet Central Asia,* 35–57. Lansing: Michigan State University Press.

Kang, David. 2009. "Between Balancing and Bandwagoning: South Korea's Response to China." *Journal of East Asian Studies* 9 (1): 1–28.

Kuik, Cheng-Chwee. 2008. "The Essence of Hedging: Malaysia and Singapore's Response to a Rising China." *Contemporary Southeast Asia* 30 (2): 159–185.

Laclau, Ernesto; Mouffe, Chantal. 2001. *Hegemony and Socialist Strategy: Towards a Radical Democratic Politics.* London: Verso.

Laruelle, Marlene, and Sebastien Peyrouse. 2012. *The Chinese Question in Central Asia: Domestic Order, Social Change and the Chinese Factor.* London: Hurst.

Liu, Kang, and Yun-Han Chu. 2014. "China's Rise Through World Public Opinion: Editorial Introduction." *Journal of Contemporary China* 24 (92): 197–202.

Maxwell, McCombs, and Donald L. Shaw. 1972. "The Agenda-Setting Function of Mass Media." *Public Opinion Quarterly* 36: 176–187.

Mearsheimer, John J. 2010. "The Gathering Storm: China's Challenge to US Power in Asia." *The Chinese Journal of International Politics* 3: 381–396.

MediaLaw Internews Project. 2010. The History of Formation of the Information Market in Kazakhstan. September 7. http://medialaw.asia/node/9139.

Ministry of Information and Culture of Kazakhstan Statistics. 2012. http://blogs.egov.kz/kulmuhamed_m/questions/195323.

O'Neill, Daniel C. 2014. "Risky Business: The Political Economy of Chinese Investment in Kazakhstan." *Journal of Eurasian Studies* 5 (2): 145–156.

Sadovskaya, Elena Y. 2007. "Chinese Migration to Kazakhstan: A Silk Road for Cooperation or a Thorny Road for Prejudice?" *China and Eurasia Forum Quarterly* 5 (4): 147–170.

Schoen, Douglas E., and Melik Kaylan. 2014. *The Russia-China Axis: The New Cold War and America's Crisis of Leadership.* New York: Encounter Books.

Shambaugh, David, and Michael Yahuda, eds. 2008. *International Relations of Asia.* Lanham: Rowman & Littlefield.

Spehr, Scott, and Nargis Kassenova. 2012. "Kazakhstan: Constructing Identity in a Post-Soviet Society." *Asian Ethnicity* 13 (2): 135–151.

Surucu, Cengiz. 2005. *Western in Form, Eastern in Content: Negotiating Time and Space in Post-Soviet Kazakhstan*. The Oxford Society for the Caspian and Central Asia. TOSCCA Online Publications. http://www.toscca.co.uk/publications.htm.

Syroezhkin, Konstantin. 2009. "Social Perceptions of China and the Chinese: A View from Kazakhstan." *Journal of Eurasian Studies* 7 (1): 29–46.

Syroezhkin, Konstantin. 2014. *Should Kazakhstan Be Afraid of China: Myths and Phobias of Bilateral Relations*. Almaty: Institute of World Economics and Politics under the Foundation of the First President of the Republic of Kazakhstan.

Wanta, Wayne, Guy Golan, and Cheolhan Lee. 2004. "Agenda Setting and International News: Media Influence on Public Perception." *Journalism and Mass Communication Quarterly* 81 (2): 364–377.

Yemelianova, Galina M. 2014. "Islam, National Identity and Politics in Contemporary Kazakhstan." *Asian Ethnicity* 15 (3): 286–301.

Zardykhan, Zharmukhamed. 2004. "Russians in Kazakhstan and Demographic Change: Imperial Legacy and the Kazakh Way of National Building." *Asian Ethnicity* 5 (1): 61–79.

Ziegler, Charles E., and Menon Rajan. 2014. "Neomercantilism and Great-Power Energy Competition in Central Asia and the Caspian." *Strategic Studies Quarterly* 8 (2): 17–41.

The discourse of racialization of labour and Chinese enterprises in Africa

Barry Sautman[a] and Yan Hairong[b]

[a]Division of Social Science, Hong Kong University of Science & Technology, Kowloon, Hong Kong; [b]Department of Applied Social Science, Hong Kong Polytechnic University, Kowloon, Hong Kong

ABSTRACT

A 'race' and labour conjunction has been theorized based on Global North investment in the Global South. Chinese enterprising in Africa allows us to analyse it in a South-South setting. Contrary to dominant discourses, Chinese employers are not the sole racializers of the African/Chinese interface. Chinese and Africans, employers and employees, as well as Western actors, co-constitute racialization, with varied consequences for each. Rhetorical racialization of African employees by some Chinese employers and African employee and politicians' racialization of Chinese, show that South-South racializations of labour markedly differ from the North-South exemplar.

Introduction

Chinese 'going out' (走出 去) to invest in Africa is discursively constructed by Western sources as 'a Manichean binary – "predator or partner", "friend or foe", "comrade or colonizer"' (Wasserman 2012). In titles of Western books on China/Africa, 'Africa is subordinate, China is the predator' (Prashad 2013). In problematizing Chinese investment in Africa, mainstream discourse attributes key issues to Chinese racialization of Africans (French 2014).

Racialized ideas of difference and hierarchy do affect Chinese enterprises in Africa, though not mainly as set out in Western-derived discourse. They theoretically situate questions such as: why, how, and from who does difference and hierarchy emerge to make 'race' a category at Chinese firms in Africa? What consequences flow for sources of racialization? How does racialization figure in politicians' and media imaginings of 'Chinese neocolonialism' (Obama 2013) and in Chinese exasperation at being singled out for criticism over their presence in Africa? (Reuters 2013).

We examine the sources, manifestations and consequences of this discourse in the African–Chinese labour relationship. Our findings augment those of scholars who analyse racialization in developed countries and racializations of labour at Western firms in developing states. We conclude that another mode exists, in which employers and employees from developing countries racialize each other.

The concept of racialization

Racialization extends racial meaning to social practices or groups, designates groups to be subjected to unequal treatment, and socio-culturally constructs hierarchy (Omi and Winant 1994, 14; Song 2004). A British ethnicity specialist has observed that

> The belief that humans belong in races was an invention of the Anglo-Saxon Protestant West that has been spread wherever it had influence. In this sense, Westerners have made races … The contemporary mode of racialization is a way of claiming that the relative privilege and disprivilege of such groups derives in part from earlier misrepresentations of their biological distinctiveness. (Banton 2005)

Sociologist Robert Miles, analysed white reactions to post-war New Commonwealth migrants to Britain. He found that UK elites legitimated a discourse of supposed intellectual incapacity and irresponsibility that upheld menial, super-low wage employment for Pakastani and Caribbean workers (Miles 1982, 167–169). Racialization was use of physical and cultural characteristics to justify adverse reactions to migrants and super-exploit their labour (Kemp 2004). It was not natural, but 'structurally determined, politically organized, and ideologically inflected … within relations of domination and subordination' (Green and Carter 1988).

The role of racializers Miles described scarcely applies to Chinese in Africa however. They are migrants at sufferance, subject to local political and social forces, and citizens of a country with a non-interference policy. Chinese and Africans may foreground cultural difference to rhetorically construct racialized hierarchies but, as a business journal reports, 'Chinese immigrants in Africa chuckle at the idea that they could lord it over the locals' (China Sub-Saharan 2015). In some 450 interviews of Chinese and African employers and employees in a dozen countries,[1] we found no Chinese and almost no African who thinks differently. These interviews, surveys of 350 Chinese in Zambia and 2,000 African university students and faculty in 10 countries, plus documentary research, are the evidential basis for arguing that the discourse of race among Chinese at enterprises in Africa is generally different from the one found by others for Global North enterprises in the Global South.

Either whole groups or discrete issues may be racialized. Mexican-Americans have been 'racialized as a dehumanized and vulnerable out-group' and 'moved steadily away from their middle position in the economic hierarchy toward the formation of an underclass' (Massey 2009). Malaysia has Malay majority/Chinese minority tensions and Malay Muslims regard contact with pigs as unclean; their elites' 'criticizing the practices of Chinese pig farmers and their "relation" with pigs [is] a covert way to racialize an entire community' (Neo 2012). Health care reform is racialized in the US. When Bill Clinton proposed it the 1990s, reform had strong support among whites and blacks, but when Barack Obama associated with it, support dropped sharply among whites, who then saw it as mainly benefitting blacks (Tesler 2012). On 'ethnic gang-related incidents', Australian media echo the police in racializing African refugees as the 'problem group', even where Africans are victims of racial violence (Windle 2008). Racialization of Chinese in Africa has proceeded from issues, such as pay and workplace safety, to Western and local political forces taking up the cudgels against 'the Chinese' as a whole.

Groups can be both racialized and ethnicized. In Chicago, 'When compared with long-time white residents, Chinese Americans are racialized as "inassimilable foreigners". When compared with poor African Americans and Latinos, however, Chinese Americans are ethnicized as the "model minority"'(Lan 2006). Many Africans racialize Chinese as more 'foreign' than whites and Indians, but some also see Chinese as models of industriousness.

Employers and not just employees can be racialized. Thus, in Los Angeles,

> Employers are not the only ones who hold strong racial-ethnic preferences and prejudices. Latina domestic workers readily agreed on who were their worst employers: Armenians, Iranians, Asians, Latinos, Blacks and Jews ... Anyone marked as nonwhite, it seems, is at risk of being denounced as a cheap, abusive, oppressive employer, to be avoided at all costs.

These immigrant workers absorb US biases of Jews as cheap, Chinese as bossy, blacks as lazy, etc., and racialize employers from groups seen as not American or white. Workers who disagree with that view are 'drowned out by the louder, frequently blanket condemnations [of] other Latina domestic workers ... ' (Hondagneu-Sotelo 2001, 57–60). Some Africans also dissent from racializing Chinese, but local politicians press for a consensus that 'the Chinese' are a problem.

Chinese have a recent, tenuous presence in Africa and lack political power, determinative influence, or cultural hegemony. They are not positioned to create a public discourse to inferiorize their African hosts, who can regulate, racialize or even expel Chinese. They cannot engage in racially disparate treatment without also crossing the Chinese state, which needs African political support (Sautman 2015). Racialization in the Chinese/African interface thus differs from racialization within developed states.

Sources of racialization in the African/Chinese interface

Racialization at Chinese firms in Africa is co-constituted by Chinese employers and workers in Africa; Chinese in China; Africans at Chinese companies; African politicians, media, and intellectuals; and their Western counterparts. Their perspectives and actions form 'overlapping racializations [in which] there are multiple levels of complexity in interracial relations, which may involve both confrontation and collaboration' (Lan 2006, 33).

Western discourse attributes racialization to *Chinese employers* even before they have any relations with African employees, as it charges Chinese with an ethnic nepotistic refusal to hire Africans (McGreal 2014). Most Chinese-owned firms however have localized workforces, despite skills shortages even in Africa's more developed countries (Sautman and Yan 2015). While among thousands of Chinese employers in Africa, racializers can be found, a US journalist notes that 'Chinese racism [is] a largely rhetorical phenomenon'. A Taiwan migrant to apartheid-era South Africa, who now owns a logistics firm with 1,000 employees (5 of them Chinese), whispered to us about his black workers that 'You can take them out of the jungle, but you can't take the jungle out of them'. The phrase is common among racists, yet, there is no indication that his company, which has black managers, practices discrimination (XXX 2014). A textile factory manager in Zambia told us a rhyme about Africans: 'On their bodies are three pieces of cloth; their economy relies on aid; to eat they rely on fruit from trees, and they say work can wait until "tomorrow" (身上三块布, 经济靠援助, 吃饭靠大树, 工作 tomorrow)'. This same boss however had a structural, non-essentializing explanation of African/Chinese work culture differences: that Africans live for the moment due to life expectancies cut short by diseases (Che Ming 2008).

Chinese in Africa seldom racialize based on the biological or meta-cultural notions that Western figures elaborate, such as veteran *New York Times* science editor Nicholas Wade's assertion that Africans' genes account for 'variations in their nature, such as their time preference, work ethic and propensity to violence' (Mailonline 2014), or French President Nicolas Sarkozy's claim that a lack of a future orientation means 'the African has not fully entered into history' (Reuters 2007). Rather, Chinese racialization rests on the concept of 'quality' or *suzhi* (素质), conceived in terms of discipline, honesty, industriousness and skill. It is applied across ethnic lines, but is sometimes generalized to groups (Yan 2014). For example, Chinese employers may speak of African laziness, but define it in terms of comparative work intensity, apply it also to Europeans, other non-Africans, and Chinese of certain regions, and see it as mutable (Sautman and Yan 2014a).

Some *Chinese workers* also racialize Africans, obviating solidarity with coworkers whose conditions may overlap with their own. Indeed, Chinese factory workers in Africa are often 'forced to work excessively long hours

... without overtime pay [and have] accommodations that are often dirty, cramped, and heavily monitored' (Rogers 2012).

In *China itself*, official discourse is more positive about Africa than anything official in the West. President Hu Jintao (2007) stated that 'The people of China and Africa have created great and brilliant cultures in the long course of history and made important contributions to the civilization and progress of mankind'. Chinese political elites have 'a sense that China needs Africa' (Chan 2014) and Chinese Africanists say that 'China needs Africa more than Africa needs China' (Liu and Li 2013). Yet, Western-derived conceptions of Africans and reverberations from experiences of Chinese returned from Africa also affect attitudes in China towards Africans, producing a spectrum of perspectives – some racializing – that influence Chinese who migrate to Africa (Bodomo 2012).

African elites, like their Western counterparts historically, may portray Chinese as alien, unassimilable and low on a status hierarchy that is often topped by whites (Almaguer 1994, 144–151; Cosmic Yoruba 2012; Sautman 2014). Some Africans, who share language, religion and other cultural elements with Europeans, see themselves as intermediate between whites and Chinese. A veteran political figure told us many Zambians

identify with Westerners and take on their prejudices. All these are self-interested. Messages coming out of Washington, London and Paris about the Chinese presence in Africa have led to cultivation of prejudices against Chinese among some Africans who identify with the West. This prejudice is also cultivated by political forces in Zambia. (Lewanika 2007)

African elites may racialize Chinese out of self-regard, to fulfil economic or electoral purposes, or to boost ties with the West. A Romanian Africanist has related that

some of the most important businessmen in Tanzania and Kenya are affected by the Chinese firms operating in this part of Africa. These owners have many political connections and are now pressing the local mass media to write about the Chinese community in negative terms. Two businessmen told me they actually ordered inflammatory articles against the Chinese community. (Codrin 2009)

Anti-Chinese agitation by political elites in African states is mostly through oppositions, but several African officials have done likewise: Zambia's (white) Vice President Guy Scott stated that Chinese 'have a reputation for being somewhat inhumane ... They are terrible managers. You get open conflict quite a bit' (Bannerman 2012). He did not mention his own party's years of anti-Chinese incitement or Zambian workers' strikes against employers of varied nationalities.

Many *African workers* at Chinese enterprises are employed by firms much less profitable than those owned by non-Chinese (Brooks 2010, 126; Sautman and Yan 2013). They may react to lower wages or anti-Chinese political mobilizations by racializing their employers or Chinese generally (Sautman and Yan 2014b), obscuring systemic causes of their problems. 'White-owned' mines in Zambia have had 'plenty of poor practice' (Lungu and Fraser 2008), but a union chairman at a Chinese-owned mine there told us 'Chinese, sorry, are not good investors, but white people are very good … In China, you have too many people, so if someone dies, you don't care' (Mwale 2011). Some African workers call for Chinese to be driven out (AFP 2014); yet, no anti-British campaigns occurred after South African police killed 34 miners striking UK-owned Lonmin in 2012, even though a Lonmin director had pushed police to act (News 4 2014). As British Africa/China scholar Giles Mohan has noted, 'No one says that the "the British" do this and the "Americans"; do that, but it is easy to put the Chinese under one label and say "the Chinese" are all this and that' (CD 2015).

Westerners antagonistic to China's political system are also a source of racialization of Chinese. They paint them as generally racist (Anderlini 2014) as Africa's worst employers (HRW 2011, 24; but see Shelton and Kabemba 2012, 170–171; Sautman and Yan 2012) and, by ignoring the presence of Chinese workers in Africa, as a neo-colonial *herrenvolk*. Thus, Western media photographic representations show only Chinese as bosses in Africa, standing arms folded while Africans do hard labour. Chinese workers are often mischaracterized as bosses: when rioting miners murdered a Chinese at Zambia's Collum Coal Mine in 2012, Western media turned that worker from a surveyor into a manager (Sautman and Yan 2014b). Yet, Western politicians and media also claim ethnocentric Chinese managers constitute their work forces solely from Chinese (Versi 2014). Illogically then, Chinese in Africa are all bosses, yet only hire Chinese workers.

Western discourse depicts only Chinese as treating Africans as inferiors. A *New York Times* journalist has stated that at Chinese firms, 'the everyday workplace is riven with accusations of mistreatment of African laborers by Chinese and accusations of virulent racism that seems to contradict the Chinese image of discretion and humility' (Hurt 2009). A UK *Sunday Times* article put it that at Chinese firms in Africa there is 'racism, a total disregard for human rights, and the sort of indifference to labor conditions that belongs in the Nineteenth Century' (Sheridan 2013). Such statements reflect no research by those who make them, but only writings of other Western journalists (Cardenal and Araujo 2012; Michel and Beuret 2009). They exemplify what an African wrote in response to a former UK diplomat's accusation that Chinese managers in Africa despise and maltreat African workers: 'Since African and Caribbean countries started turning away from Europe towards China … many white people keep bleating on about how Chinese might be more racist than Europeans' (JesusFan 2009). A detailed, critical examination of labour relations at Chinese firms in Africa in fact recounts no acts of 'virulent racism' (Baah and Jauch 2009). A study of relations between Chinese traders and their Ghanaian employees concluded that 'Chinese traders rarely engage in active racial discrimination. This is demonstrated in their almost egalitarian behavior towards employees and members of the lower social strata, such as female head porters' (Giese 2013).

Scholars allude to Chinese 'casual racism' (Brautigam 2013) or 'harmonious racism' (Shih 2013, 33–41) without indicating whether other actors construct race in Africa. Rracialization does however affect many non-Chinese workplaces: white-owned South African supermarket chain Shoprite is ubiquitous in neighbouring states, but senior managers are mainly white (Miller 2005, 9). Kansanshi and Lumwana, Canadian-owned mines near Solwezi, Zambia, each have 200–300 expats (FQM 2012; Williams 2012). At Kansanshi,

> The company has built homes, pools, a gymnasium, and even a golf course, but to the annoyance of workers and Solwezi residents, these are for the use of those high up on the mine's organizational structure. Given that there is a degree of overlap between race and the division of labor at the mine, these words of a Kansanshi worker are perfectly understandable: 'This is apartheid ... Kansanshi has created a new Cape Town'. This discursive connection is all the more pertinent because many expatriate managers at Kansanshi are from South Africa. (Negi 2012, 35)

Zambia's Minister of Commerce has received complaints that at Kansanshi, more qualified Zambians 'perform duties for inexperienced and unqualified expatriates who get huge salaries at their expense' (Steel Guru 2011).

Some Western sources directly urge African elites to racialize Chinese in Africa. A report for US government-funded Freedom House called on Zambia's government to single out Chinese for exclusion (Lasner 2011). That approach accords with US-created notions of strategic rivalry with China that resemble the sense of 'racial urgency' that Western elites advanced in the early and late twentieth Century vis-à-vis Japan, and with Western racial stereotypes of Chinese (Kowner 2013).

The causes and consequences of Chinese racialization of Africans, as well as African and Western racializations of Chinese are thus varied. Our interviews, surveys and the works of other scholars indicate however that all these actors participate in racializing the African/Chinese interface.

The concept of racialization of labour

Racialization of labour is

> everyday production, reproduction, and contest over racialized meanings and structures implicated in the production of notions of skill, in employers' everyday assessments of good and bad workers, and in a range of institutional practices that reproduce both the racialized division of labour and racialized job and occupational hierarchies. (Maldonado 2006, 353)

It aims at 'exploit[ing] workers at higher rates under worse conditions, usually for worse pay'. Most seafarers are 'men of color from the Global South' who 'experience unfair treatment due to their race or nationality', including low wages, physical abuse, and a bar on contacting unions. Gradients of racialized exploitation also exist: highly trained Chinese seafarers are paid on average 20 per cent less than Filipinos, the world's largest contingent of seafarers (Bonacich and Wilson 2008, 170–171) Latino day labourers rebuilding post-Hurricane Katrina New Orleans were subordinated to white and black workers (Murga 2011). Racialization of labour also occurs when workers demean those of another 'race' by discursive marginalization (Wilson 2008).

Racialization of labour is often framing of racially disparate citizenship rights and levels of labour exploitation, as employers naturalize workers of one group as well-suited to a kind of labour, but others as lazy or incompliant (Maldonado 2009). It can involve societal divisions of labour embedded in political systems. The nineteenth century US's 'race-labor hierarchy' had free white labour on top, then 'degraded' Chinese indentured servitude, black slavery, and Mexican peonage (Phan 2004). Southern and eastern European workers were also viewed as inferior compared to northern Europeans (Roediger and Esch 2012, 90). Pre-Second World War productivity differential studies in France put ethnic groups 'in a predictable sequence [that] privileged whiteness and proximity to French people' (Camiscioli 2008, 70–73).

Naturalization of work suitability by ethnicity and citizenship produces hierarchies. In the early 2000s California food industry, white workers averaged U$14.46 an hour; US-born Latinos earned $10.92. Latinos of diverse immigration status in California's tortilla industry earned $8.79 an hour; but the Mexican citizens of Tiajuana's tortilla industry got $1.69 (Munoz 2008). In Colombia's cut flower industry, workers in 2005 earned $0.48 per hour and were people of colour labouring at export-oriented plantations owned locally or by US and other transnational firms. Owners and managers were from the European-descended middle and upper classes (Sanmiguel-Valderrama 2007).

Edna Bonacich et al., whose theorization we augment, conceive racialization of labour as whites benefitting by denying rights to peoples of colour. Primary racialization by employers creates more effective exploitation through lower wages and worse conditions than those provided white workers. Secondary racialization results from white workers' fear of displacement by subordinated workers. The concept is exemplified by US employers and workers deeming Chinese workers 'not equal human beings' and 'faceless hordes of working machines', who gratefully receive low wages, steal US jobs, lower labour standards, and eschew struggle. Bonacich et al. also posit that while US workers have imperfect rights, Global South workers 'lack citizenship rights in relation to international capital' by not being allowed to organize. Even workers at US-outsourced call centers in India, who have better than average conditions, are racialized labour, because their wages are a tenth those of comparable US workers and they are forced to imitate Americans (Bonacich, Alimahomed, and Wilson 2008).

A South-South racialization of labour?

Chinese racialization at firms in Africa lacks most characteristics set out for North-South invested enterprises. Even the rhetoric differs. Unlike the Americans Bonacich discusses in relation to workers in China, Chinese in Africa do not conceive that Africans workers are grateful for low wages or steal their home country jobs, lower labour standards, or shun struggle. They view labour standards in some African states as higher than in China (Ke 2011), (Beijing Laodi 2013), Africans as more likely than Chinese to insist on respect for labour standards (Wong 2013), and some African countries as having wage requirements higher than in China (Qu 2013). Our interviews show that unlike Westerners in developing states, Chinese in Africa do not think they benefit from political or labour rights that Africans lack and that Chinese firms do not demand African employees conform to Chinese culture, even as to work ethic.[2]

Bonacich's racialization of labour concept involves whites profiting from racializing non-whites, but not non-whites of one developing country racializing workers or employers of another one. It does not concern workers in one developing country, employed by firms from another, who have the same or better rights and wages than workers in the firms' country of origin. Chinese firms in Africa may pay Chinese more than locals, due to differences in skill and experience and a need to incentivize work far from home (Baah and Jauch 2009, 70, 115, 151, 181, 194–195, 221, 330). Many however do not pay Africans less than what comparable workers earn in China. Our 2014 surveys of Chinese-owned firms' Zambian copper miners and workers at China's largest copper mine, found Zambians out-earned Chinese by US$640–555 a month. At two Western-owned mines, Zambians averaged $703 a month, yet developed country miners average much more: US$5,300 in Canada (Caldwell 2014). Chinese at their companies in Africa do not necessarily earn more than like-qualified Africans at non-Chinese firms. Chinese mining engineers in Zambia in 2011 were paid $10,000 a year (Brautigam 2011, 6), less than Zambian engineers at a major mine owned by a UK-based firm (Servant 2009). In 2007, 'Chinese engineers in Angola [were] paid only one-sixth of what Angolans can expect from European [-owned] firms' (Song 2007). Chinese workers building Angola's Benguela Railway received $150–250 a month (Grobler 2014), while Angolan construction workers earn $250–500 a month (Thanh Nien News 2014), a pay difference inconceivable for Western expatriate workers.

Chinese tend to not concentrate in super-low wage African countries, except Ethiopia. Perhaps half of Chinese in Africa reside in its largest manufacturer, South Africa (Li 2013), which received 35 per cent of all Chinese investment in Africa from 2001 to 2012 (Copley 2014). Its 2014 manufacturing wage averaged US$1,200 – much higher, for example, than Zambia's average of $165–200 (Davis 2014) – while China's was $560 (Hamlin 2014). There are some 20 whites for each Chinese in South Africa and on average they earn 6 times what blacks do (Laing 2012). In 2011, whites were 12 per cent of economically active South Africans, but 65 per cent of all top managers, 73 per cent of top private sector managers and 69–72 per cent of senior managers (Commission 2012). Chinese, however, are economically intermediate. With whites much more numerous and economically dominant than Chinese, socioeconomic differences between blacks and Chinese hardly figure in South Africa's racial hierarchy (Huynh, Park, and Chen 2010).

The concept of racialization of labour also does not presently deal with (mostly) non-self-segregating foreign employers. Some Chinese live in group accommodations, due to company concern about personal safety (Kairu 2015) and those who speak only Chinese cannot much interact with locals. Most Chinese in Africa however do not 'seal themselves off from the societies around them as best they can' (McNamee 2012), as they do not work for firms with 'compounds', but live among and interact with locals (Giese 2011; Oreglia 2012, 9). Chinese are the second-largest foreign group in Equatorial Guinea. The largest is Americans, who

> live in private compounds far from Equatoguinean towns. Unlike the Americans, Chinese immigrants live among the Equatoguinean people and have constant economic interaction with them in different ways, such as providing products and services for them, working for them, renting business premises and accommodation from them [and] employing them. (Esteban 2009, 682)

Asked by a US reporter about the Chinese community in Congo's Kinshasa, a local journalist replied

> There is no Chinese community; they live with us. They live right next door to me. They eat with us, they shop with us … They're learning Lingala … and, most importantly, they are not afraid of us … We joke among ourselves that the Chinese skin is becoming browner and browner to where it's now black. (Olander 2010)

A Nigerian blogger, responding to a former US Ambassador's assertion that Chinese in Africa segregate themselves, wrote:

> Are they less 'segregated' from Africans than Westerners? Yes … the Chinese are more likely to live among and shop in the same markets as Africans … I have a couple of Chinese neighbors, but almost no Westerner lives on the Lagos 'mainland' … and some Westerners don't even look through their windows when being driven around. They live in gilded ghettos for 'expatriates' … 99% have no local friends, despise the locals, and minimize interaction with locals. (MrOkadaman28 2012)

Well-off Chinese reside in upscale African neighbourhoods, but employers and workers of modest means live in much poorer areas (AFP 2015; Shinn and Eisenberg 2012, 222). A Namibian trader in Swokupmund told us that

> The Chinese are much better than the Germans or the Boers. The Chinese live, work, and walk among us, as opposed to the whites, who live only in town in their big, fancy houses. The local whites warn white tourists to stay out of the townships; that the Namibians are all thieves ... but the Chinese do not look down on us. They take local taxis; even the wealthier Chinese still take taxis. (Nzoh 2008)

In Sudan, some firms encourage Chinese employees to learn Arabic (Mao 2008) and a Sudanese manager has said that in his factory

> Sudanese ... eat from one big plate – while Chinese eat from their individual bowls. But Chinese have learned to eat with Sudanese in one group ... In the factory, if Chinese are invited to eat with Sudanese in a group, the Chinese do not refuse to do so. (Mekki 2008)

In Zambia, a leading intellectual has said of Chinese

> They're ready to go deep into all sectors of society where there have been only Zambians. So they are unlike Westerners ... We can say that Chinese have assimilated in Zambian better than the Europeans, who've come here with raised noses. Chinese have become more easily integrated. (Saasa 2014)

A Zambian political figure averred that 'Compared to Europeans, Chinese will do manual work. No white boss complex. Whatever they ask Africans to do, Chinese themselves also do. There is nothing that's beneath the Chinese. This is very refreshing to Africans' (Lewanika 2008). A Nambian journalist has written that 'The Chinese are indeed not living in mansions with an army of African domestics. They dig, shovel, saw, clear and carry away the rubble themselves, instead of standing around raving sharp orders to African workers' (Akinyi 2008, 85). A Zambian human resources officer at Chinese-owned Chambishi Copper Smelter said

> The Chinese are very simple. At the staff canteen, they even wash their own dishes. The CEO wears a worksuit. The CEO also goes to staff canteen and lines up to get his food. In fact, 80% of Chinese wear work suits. I think it's good because workers don't feel so much status. (Kabende 2012)

Zambians who have worked under a succession of Indian, Swiss and Chinese firms at Luanshya Copper Mine (LCM) have said that Chinese are more apt than other employers to have friendly relations with them. A miner told us that 'Chinese mingle with us. Indians never do that. Nor would South African Boers' (Sikapoko 2013). Another recalled that in contrast to Chinese, 'Under the [Swiss] owners, there were a lot of Boers working at LCM who used a lot of abusive curse language that used to cause frictions'

(Zulu 2012). The firm's Zambian Head Geologist recalled that 'The Boers would kick you' and, before that,

> The Indian way of management's approach to other races [was] not OK. They just command you and sideline you. Chinese are willing to learn, no matter how many degrees they have ... Indian [managers] don't want to talk to lower classes. Chinese will sit with you and ask you, if we do this, what do you think? (Mubita 2013)

The Kenyan programme head of a German NGO in Nairobi told us that 'Chinese are actually regarded as more flexible employers than either Indians or whites and even than some black Kenyan employers' (Gikang'a 2007). A Tanzanian who had studied in Nanjing and worked as a translator in Dar Es Salaam related that

> Chinese tend to live among Africans, while Westerners tend to have their own enclaves ... Chinese live where they work or close to it, while Westerners feel that where they live should be separate from where they work ... those Chinese who work with Tanzanians on an everyday basis would be forced by circumstances to speak Swahili and to live with local people and conditions. (Mateza 2006)

Most Chinese have far less cultural overlap with Africans than do Western expats, yet do not generally display the aloofness that scholars of racialization of labour note at developed country enterprises in the Global South. Those Chinese who go further than Western expats in interacting with Africans may have more modest economic positions or a different sense of 'race', one owing to China's socialist legacy or to a sense that China is a developing country.

The public views of elites about how particular 'races' labour often differ from their actual appraisals. Pre-Civil War US Southern white elites crafted what was, in effect, an official view that blacks were 'shiftless'. In their writings on managing slaves however, slaveholders objectively appraised black workers as more productive than whites (Roediger and Esch 2012). Southern planters tried replacing freed slaves with white immigrants and Chinese after the war, but found them not sufficiently hardworking or disciplined and reverted to African-American labour (Follett 2011). British elites officially advanced a racialized discourse of inferior 'Lascar' (Asian) seamanship, but UK marine experts held that Lascars were as good sailors as any (Hyslop 2014). China has long officially viewed Africans as hardworking and its Africa specialists regard African women as particularly so (Liu 2012; Yang 2002; Zhou 2013). It is Chinese managers who hold mixed views of Africans as workers: some fault their work habits; others are praiseful. A construction firm boss wrote:

> Often our African foremen would outperform the Chinese foremen .... We were far more wary of our ambitious Chinese staff than the Africans, who were

generally more consistent .... [O]ur African workers are also hard workers for our company .... Many of our African staff who have served us well for decades were nurtured and promoted by the company for displaying that 'sense of urgency' on the job, despite their base education. (KF 2013)

Chinese factory bosses in Ethiopia especially appreciate the 'hardworking and quick at learning' women workers (Shen 2013, 20). Chinese factory manager Lao Yang has said in a 2008 letter to Sudanese managers of Khartoum's Anyang Battery Factory, 'Sudanese are not lazy. You just need good management practices'.

Even Chinese managers not impressed by African work intensity praise other attributes. A machinery engineering firm manager in Sudan has called it is a 'civilized country' of trustworthy, linguistically talented people (Zhao 2007). A Chinese operations manager at Zambia's Chambishi Mine has said local workers there are more polite, more reliable, better at following orders, and have a higher 'level of civilization' than Chinese (Zhou 2008). A Chinese agriculture machinery firm and chain store owner in Zambia avers that some local employees are very smart and entrepreneurs hardworking; Zambians are also more inclined than Chinese to follow rules and procedures, from which Chinese should learn (Han 2014).

Chinese employers' view of Africans is not racialized in a general sense and their practice even less so, while racialization of Chinese by some Africans, especially politicians, and by Western elites, is not uncommon. That configuration raises the question of whether existing concepts of racialization of labour, arising from North-South interaction, should be augmented to account for the markedly different role of 'race' at Chinese enterprises in Africa.

Conclusion: the mitigation of racialization of labour

Why might racialization of labour at Chinese enterprises in Africa differ from the North-South scenario? Not merely because China is a developing country: our interviews indicate racialization at Indian and 'white' mining firms in Zambia have many commonalities. More likely it is because the Chinese government demands that enterprises take into account China's relations with African states. Chinese are also more inclined than most peoples to oppose racial discrimination. A University of Maryland poll in 16 countries found that

The Chinese are among the publics with the greatest support for the importance of equal treatment for different races and ethnicities, second only to Mexicans among the publics polled. China also has the second-largest majority rejecting employers having the right to discriminate based on race or ethnicity, and are among the largest majorities that favor their government making efforts to prevent racial and ethnic discrimination. (WorldPublicOpinion.Org. 2008)

Chinese firms can thus be made to mitigate the existing, largely rhetorical racialization of labour and avoid actions perceived as racially tinged. When a riot-induced shooting by Chinese supervisors occurred at the Collum Coal Mine in 2010, wounding 13 Zambians, the Chinese Embassy pressured the mine's Australian Chinese owner to apologize, pay compensation, and alter work conditions (Sautman and Yan 2014b). When in 2015 a Chinese restaurant in Nairobi curtailed nighttime service for some black customers, the Chinese Embassy condemned it (Capitalfm 2015).

There is a second basis for mitigating the racialization of labour: the failure of Africa's most notorious anti-Chinese campaign. After becoming Zambia's President, anti-Chinese agitator Michael Sata acknowledged that 'When we were campaigning … I promised I will sort the Chinese out. They are also going to sort me out' (Sata's U-turn 2011). Reuter's Africa bureau chief, asked after Sata's death in 2014 about his 'relationship with the Chinese', responded that 'there was really nothing concrete that emerged from his rhetoric, in terms of policy toward China' (Cropley 2014). Sata's racializing of Chinese helped bring him to power, but brought little gain to Zambian workers; he ended up firing striking nurses and imposing hiring and wage freezes (President Lungu 2015).

Political forces operating from inside and outside the continent will doubtless continue to racialize Chinese in Africa. Africa however is not like Mongolia or Vietnam, where nationalist narratives can focus exclusively on China (Bille 2015; Two Brothers 2015). Many Africans know that the US and old colonial powers have much greater influence on the continent than China does. Africans are also not untouched by class-oriented approaches. These are re-emerging under conditions of ever-deepening neo-liberalization and inequality, as the birth of new political forces in South Africa attest (Buccus 2015). Racialization of labour thus exists in the Chinese/African interface, but whether increasing African/Chinese contact will aggravate or attenuate it remains to be seen.

Notes

1. Botswana, China, Egypt, Ethiopia, Ghana, Kenya, Namibia, South Africa Sudan, Tanzania, Zambia, Zimbabwe. Our interviews and surveys were part of Hong Kong's Research Grants Council-funded projects on Chinese investment and localization of Chinese enterprises in Africa.
2. Compare Wong (1999) (employer demands conformity to Japanese cultural norms from its Hong Kong employees).

Disclosure statement

No potential conflict of interest was reported by the authors.

Funding

This work was supported by Hong Kong Research Grants Council [grant number 641113].

References

AFP (Agence France Presse). 2014. "Chinese Sugar Firm Seeks Compensation From Madagascar After Riots." December 16.

AFP. 2015. "Chinese Become Targets in DR Congo Anti-Government riots." January 25.

Akinyi Princess of K'Orinda-Yimbo. 2008. *Darkest Europe and Africa's Nightmare: A Critical Observation of Neighboring Continents*. New York: Algora.

Almaguer, Thomas. 1994. *Racial Fault Lines: The Historical Origins of White Supremacy in California*. Berkeley: University of California Press.

Anderlini, Jamil. 2014. "'Rejuvenation' Aim Threatens to Harden China's Racial Attitudes." *Financial Times*, September 1.

Baah, Anthony Yaw, and Herbert Jauch. 2009. *Chinese Investments in Africa: A Labor Perspective*. Nairobi: African Labor Research Network.

Bannerman, Lucy. 2012. "Dr Scott, I presume?" *Spectator*, March 10.

Banton, Michael. 2005. "Historical and Contemporary Modes of Racialization." In *Racialization: Studies in Theory and Practice*, edited by Karim Murji and John Solomos, 51–68. Oxford: Oxford University Press.

Beijing Laodi. 2013. "Chinese are not More Civilized than Africans, China-Africa Project." August 10. www.chinaafricaproject.com/chinese-people-are-not-more-civilized-than-africans-translation/.

Bille, Franck. 2015. *Sinophobia: Anxiety, Violence and the Making of Mongolian Identity*. Honolulu: University of Hawaii.

Bodomo, Adams. 2012. *Africans in China: A Socio-Cultural Study and its Implications on Africa-China Relations*. Amherst: Cambria Press.

Bonacich, Edna, Sabrina Alimahomed, and Jake B. Wilson. 2008. "The Racialization of Global Labor." *American Behavioral Scientist* 52 (3): 342–355, 348.

Bonacich, Edna, and Jake Wilson. 2008. *Getting the Goods: Ports, Labor, and the Logistics Revolution*. Ithaca, NY: Cornell University Press.

Brautigam, Deborah. 2011. "China in Africa: Seven Myths (ARI)." Real Instituto Elcano. www.isn.ethz.ch/ Digital-Library/Publications/Detail/?lng=en&id=142931.

Brautigam, Deborah. 2013. *Sweet and Sour: China in Africa, Beyond the Headlines*. University of Melbourne, Melbourne, Australia, Up Close, January 18. http://upclose.unimelb.edu.au.

Brooks, Andrew. 2010. "Spinning and Weaving Discontent: Labor Relations and the Production of Meaning at Zambia-China Mulungushi Textiles." *Journal of Southern African Studies* 36 (1): 113–132.

Buccus, Imraan. 2015. "Why 2015 Progressive Forces Need to Build the United Front." *Sunday Independent*, January 11.

Caldwell, Jack. 2014. "Mining Salaries." *Technomine*. http://technology.infomine.com/reviews/miningsalaries/welcome.asp?view=full.

Camiscioli, Elisa. 2008. *Reproducing the French Race: Immigration, Intimacy, and Embodiment in the Early Twentieth Century*. Durham, NC: Duke University Press.

Capitalfm. 2015. "Chinese Embassy slams restaurant over racism." March 26. http://allafrica.com/stories/201503271093.html.

Cardenal, Juan Pablo, and Heriberto Araujo. 2012. *China's Silent Army: the Pioneers, Traders, Fixers and Workers are Remaking the World in Beijing's Image*. London: Allen Lane.

CD (China Daily). 2015. "Debunking Stereotypes about Chinese." January 23.

Chan, Stephen. 2014. "Stepping Stones, Quagmires and Capacity." *The Africa Report*, April 10.

Che Ming. 2008. "Managing Director, Zambia China Mulungushi Textiles." *Lusaka*, September 25.

"China/Sub-Saharan Africa Business: One among Many". 2015. *Economist*, January 17.

Codrin, Arsene. 2009. "Ten Reasons Why Chinese are Despised in Africa." *African Politics Portal*, August 5. www.african-politics.com/ten-reasons-why-chinese-are-despised-in-africa.

Commission for Employment Equity. 2012. Annual Report 2011–2012. www.info.gov.za/view/DownloadFileAction? id=174047.

Copley, Amy. 2014. "The US-Africa Leaders Summit: A Focus on Foreign Direct Investment." *Brookings Institution*. www.brookings.edu/blogs/africa-in-focus/posts/2014/07/11-foreign-direct-investment-us-africa-leaders-summit.

Cosmic Yoruba. 2012. "Self-Esteem and Race in Nigeria." *This is Africa*, May 23. www.thisisafrica.me/opinion/detail/19486/Self-esteem-and-race-in-Nigeria.

Cropley, Ed. 2014. "Zambia's King Cobra Spits No More." *Biznews.com*, October 29. www.biznews.com/video/2014/10/29/zambias-king-cobra-spits-no-more-bequeaths-free-africa-its-first-white-president/ .

Davis, Kurt. 2014. "Sub-Saharan Africa Manufacturing: Where to Build a Factory?" *Venture Africa*, November 3.

Esteban, Mario. 2009. "The Chinese Amigo: Implications for the Development of Equatorial Guinea." *The China Quarterly* 199: 667–685.

Follett, Richard. 2011. "Legacies of Enslavement: Plantation Identities and the Problem of Freedom." In *Slavery's Ghost: the Problem of Freedom in the Age of Emancipation*, edited by Richard Follett, Eric Foner, and Walter Johnson, 50–84. Baltimore, MD: Johns Hopkins University Press.

FQM [First Quantum Minerals]. 2012. "Working and Living at Kansanshi." www.first-quantum.com/Careers/our-locations/zambia/working-and-living-on-kansanshi/default.aspx.

French, Howard. 2011. "Howard French on Africa in a Chinese century." *Radio Open Source*, January 21. www.radioopensource.org/howard-french-on-africa-in-a-chinese-century/.

French, Howard. 2014. *China's Second Continent: How a Million Migrants are Building a new Empire in Africa*. New York: Random House.

Giese, Karsten. 2011. "Chinese Networks in Urban West Africa." *Internationale Konferenz Migration und Kultur*, Alpen-Adria Universität. www.spp1448.de/projects/entrepreneurial-chinese-migrants/project-output/conference-presentations/.

Giese, Karsten. 2013. "Same-same but Different: Chinese Perspectives on African Labor." *The China Journal* 69: 134–153.

Gikang'a, Hezron. 2007. "Heinrich Boll Stiftung." *Nairobi*, December 20.

Green, Marci and Bob Carter. 1988. "'Races' and 'Race-Makers': The Politics of Racialization." *Sage Race Relations Abstracts* 13 (2): 4–30.

Grobler, John. 2014. "Chinese Infrastructure Lubricates Outflow of Angolan and DRC Resources." *Eurasia Review*, April 11.

Hamlin, Kevin. 2014. "Ethiopia Feels China's Huge Presence." *Sunday Independent*, July 27.

Han, Jing. 2014. "Camco." *Lusaka*, June 7.

Hondagneu-Sotelo, Pierrette. 2001. *Doméstica: Immigrant Workers Cleaning and Caring in the Shadows of Affluence*. Berkeley: University of California Press.

HRW [Hurman Rights Watch]. 2011. "'You'll be Fired if You Refuse': labor abuses in Zambia's Chinese State-Owned Copper Mines." November 3, www.hrw.org/reports/2011/11/03/you-ll-be-fired-if-you-refuse.

Hu Jintao. 2007. "'Full Text' of Hu Jintao's Speech ... " *BBC*, February 11.

Hurt, Harry III. 2009. "China's Wide Reach in Africa." *New York Times*, July 19.

Huynh, Tu, Yoon Jung Park, and Anna Ying Chen. 2010. "Faces of China: New Chinese Migrants in South Africa: 1980s to the Present." *African and Asian Studies* 9: 286–306.

Hyslop, Jonathan. 2014. "'Ghostlike' Seafarers and Sailing Ship Nostalgia: The Figure of the Steamship Lascar in the British Imagination C.1880–1960." *Journal of Maritime Research* 16 (2): 212–228.

JesusFan. 2009. "Post to Tim Collard, "Are the Chinese Racist?" *Telegraph*, November 2. http:// tmcollardblogspot.hk/2009/11/are-chinese-racist.html.

Kabende, Martin. 2012. Kitwe. August 15.

Kairu, Pauline. 2015. "Lonely Camp Life Blamed on Thika Road's 'Chinese Babies.'" *Daily Nation*, January 26.

Ke, Shanshan. 2011. "非洲国家劳工标准对中国在非洲企业的影响 [Labor Standards of African Countries and their Impact on Chinese Enterprises: A Case Study of Zambia]." PhD diss., Zhejiang Normal University. http://www.taodocs.com/p-3686793.html.

Kemp, Adriana. 2004. "Labor Migration and Racialization: Labor Market Mechanisms and Labor Migration Control Policies in Israel." *Social Identities* 10 (2): 267–292.

KF. 2013. "Post to China in Africa the Real Story." February 5. www.chinaafricarealstory.com/2013/02/nigerian-workers-protest-conditions-at-html.

Kowner, Rotem. 2013. "Between Contempt and Fear: Western Racial Construction of East Asians since 1800." In *Race and Racism in Modern East Asia: Western and Eastern Construction*, edited by Rotem Kowner and Walter Demel, 93–126. Leiden: Brill.

Laing, Aislinn. 2012. "South Africa's Whites Still Paid Six Times More than Blacks." *Telegraph*, October 30.

Lan, Shanshan. 2006. "Chinese Americans in Multiracial Chicago: A Story of Overlapping Racializations." *Asian American Law Journal* 13: 31–55.

Lasner, Thoams. 2011. "After a Democratic Power Transfer, Zambia Must Tackle Chinese Investment Issues and Human Rights Reforms." *Freedom House*, November 15. www.freedomhouse.orblog/after-democratic-power-transfer-zambia-must-tackle-chinese-investment-issues-and-human-rights.

Lewanika, Akashambatwa. 2007. Lusaka, July 21.

Lewanika, Akashambatwa. 2008. Lusaka, July 7.

Li, Anshan. 2013. "China's African Policy and the Chinese Immigrants in Africa." In *Routledge Handbook of the Chinese Diaspora*, edited by Tan Chee-Beng, 59–75. London: Routledge.

Liu, Guangyuan. 2012. "H.E. Ambassador Liu Guangyuan's speech ... " *Chinese Embassy in Kenya*, January 11. www.fmprc. gov.cn/eng/wjb/ zwjg/zwbd/t894873.shtml.

Liu, Guijing, and Anshan Li. 2013. "刘贵今、李安山谈习近平主席出访非洲与中非关系 [Liu Guijin, Li Anshan talk of Xi Jinping's Africa trip and China-Africa relations]." 人民网, March 26. http://fangtan.people.com.cn/n/2013/0326/c147550-20924046.html.

Lungu, John, and Alastair Fraser. 2008. "For Whom the Windfalls: Winners and Losers in the Privatization of Zambia's Copper Mines." *Civil Society Trade Network of Zambia*. www.liberationafrique.org/ IMG/ ... /Minewatchzambia.php.

Mailonline, Reporter. 2014. "Race Row Over Book that Claims Africans are Prone to Violence." *Daily Mail*, August 14.

Maldonado, Maria Marta. 2006. "Racial Triangulation of Latino/a Workers by Agricultural Employers." *Human Organization* 65 (4): 353–361.

Maldonado, Maria Marta. 2009. "'It is Their Nature to do Menial Labor': The Racialization of 'Latino/a Workers' by Agricultural Employers." *Ethnic and Racial Studies* 32 (6): 1017–1036.

Mao, Lin. 2008. "Tianbao Construction." *Khartoum*, November 14.

Massey, Douglas. 2009. "Racial Formation in Theory and Practice; the Case of Mexicans in the United States." *Race and Social Problems* 1 (1): 12–26.

Mateza, Mr. 2006. Dar Es Salaam, July 9.

McGreal, Chirs. 2014. "Obama Suggests that US is Better Partner than China to African leaders." *Guardian*, August 5.

McNamee, Terence. 2012. "The Real Front Line of Chinese in Africa." *Financial Times*, May 7.

Mekki, Mr. 2008. Anyang Battery Factory, Khartoum, November 23.

Michel, Serge and Michel Beuret. 2009. *China Safari: On the Trail of Beijing's Expansion in Africa*. New York: Nation Books.

Miles, Robert. 1982. *Racism and Migrant Labor*. London: Routledge.

Miller, Darlene. 2005. "White Managers and the African Renaissance: A 'Retail Renaissance' or a New Colonial Encounter at South African Companies in Foreign, African Countries." *Codresia*. www.codesria.org/IMG/pdf/miller.pdf.

MrOkadaman28. 2012. "John Campbell on How the Chinese are Perceived in Africa." August 7. www.youtube.com/watch?v=xqwqWOSLJuk.

Mubita, Wellington. 2013. Luanshya, June 25.

Munoz, Carolina Bank. 2008. *Transnational Tortilla: Race, Gender and Shop Floor Politics in Mexico and the United States*. Ithaca, NY: Cornell University Press.

Murga, Aurelia. 2011. "The Racialization of Day Labor Work in the U.S. Labor Market: Examining the Exploitation of Immigrant Labor." PhD diss., Texas A&M University.

Mwale, Alex. 2011. NUMAW, Chambishi Mine, Chingola, August 2011.

Negi, Rohit. 2012. "The Micropolitics of Mining and Development in Zambia." *African Studies Quarterly* 12 (2): 27–44.

Neo, Harvey. 2012. "They Hate Pigs, Chinese Farmers … Everything!: Beastly Racialization in Multiethnic Malaysia." *Antipode* 44 (3): 950–970.

News 4. 2014. "Should Ramaphosa Face Murder Charges over Marikana Massacre?" November 4.

Nzoh, Frank. 2008. Swakopmund, July 20.

Obama, Barack. 2013. "Remarks by Pres. Obama … " *White House*, June 29. www. whitehouse.gov/the-press-office/2013/06/29/remarks-president-obama-young-african-leaders-initiative-town-hall.

Olander, Eric. 2010. "Chinese: It's the New Black in Kinshasa." *China Talking Points*, February 21. www.chinatalkingpoints.com/chinese-its-the-new-black-in-kinshasa/.

Omi, Michael, and Howard Winant. 1994. *Racial Formation in the United States*. London: Routledge.

Oreglia, Elisa. 2012. "Africa's Many Chinas." *Intel Labs IXR*. www.ercolino.eu/docs/ Oreglia_Proj_ AfricasManyChinas.pdf.

Phan, Hoang Jia. 2004. "'A Race so Different': Chinese Exclusion, the Slaughterhouse Cases and Plessy V. Ferguson." *Labor History* 45 (2): 133–163.

Prashad, Vijay. 2013. "The Big BRICS: China Finds its Place." *The 4th Media*, March 28. www.4thmedia.org/2013/03/28/the-big-brics-china-finds-its-place/.

President Lungu. 2015. "Lifts Wage Freeze." *Lusaka Times*, May 1.

Qu, Xing. 2013. "Applause for China-Africa Cooperation." *Daily Mail*, April 3.

Reuters. 2007. "Africans Still Seething over Sarkozy's Speech." September 5.

Reuters. 2013 "China's Xi Tells Africa He Seeks Relationship of Equals." March 25.

Roediger, David, and Elizabeth Esch. 2012. *The Production of Difference; Race and Management of Labor in US History*. Oxford: Oxford University Press.

Rogers, Tonya. 2012. "The Center Cannot Hold: Assessing the Reach of China's Labor Protections to Migrant Workers in Africa." *Fordham International Law Journal* 35: 1075–1120.

Saasa, Oliver. 2014. Lusaka, June 6.

Sanmiguel-Valderrama, Olga. 2007. "The Feminization and Racialization of Labor in the Colombian Fresh-cut Flower Industry." *Journal of Developing Societies* 23 (1–2): 71–88.

Sata's U-turn. 2011. "On China." *Lusaka Times*, October 30.

Sautman, Barry. 2014. "The Chinese Defilement Case: Racial Profiling in an African 'Model of Democracy'." *Rutgers Race and the Law Review* 14 (1): 87–134.

Sautman, Barry. 2015. "Racialization as Agency in Zambia-China Relations." In *African Agency in China-Africa Relations*, edited by Aleksandra Gadzala, 127–148. New York: Rowman & Littlefield.

Sautman, Barry, and Yan Hairong. 2012. *The Chinese are the Worst? Human Rights and Labor Practices in Zambian Mining*. Baltimore: University of Maryland.

Sautman, Barry, and Hairong Yan. 2013. "Beginning of a World Empire? Contesting Chinese Copper Mining in Zambia." *Modern China* 39 (2): 131–164.

Sautman, Barry, and Hairong Yan. 2014a. "Chinese, Africans and the Discourse of Laziness." Paper, Chinese in Africa/Africans in China Research Network conference, Guangzhou, December 13.

Sautman, Barry, and Hairong Yan. 2014b. "Bashing 'the Chinese': Contextualizing Zambia's Collum Coal Mine Shooting." *Journal of Contemporary China 23* (90): 1073–1092. http://www.ccs.org.za/wp-content/uploads/2015/07/CCS_AEAA_01-02_June_2015.pdf.

Sautman, Barry, and Hairong Yan. 2015. "Localization of Chinese Enterprises and African Agency." *African-East Asian Affairs Special* Edition: 60–69.

Servant, Jean-Christophe. 2009. "Mined out in Zambia." *Le Monde Diplomatique*, May.

Shelton, Garth, and Claude Kabemba. 2012. "Win-Win Partnership? China, Southern Africa and the Extractive Industries." *Southern Africa Resources Watch*. www.osisa.org/sites/default/files/china-africa_web_sarw_ 0.pdf.

Shen, Xiaofang. 2013. "Private Chinese Investment in Africa: Myths and Realities." Policy Research Working Paper 6311, World Bank. http://documents.worldbank.org/curated/en/2013/01/17159618/private-chinese-investment-africa-myths-realities.

Sheridan, Michael. 2013. "Empire building." *Sunday Times*, February 3.

Shih, Chih-yu. 2013. *Sinicizing International Relations: Self, Civilization and Intellectual Politics in Subaltern East Asia*. London: Palgrave.

Shinn, David, and Joshua Eisenberg. 2012. *China and Africa: A Century of Engagement*. Philadelphia: University of Pennsylvania.

Sikapoko, Santos. 2013. China Luanshya Mine, Luanshya, June 23.

Song, Mini. 2004. "Introduction: Who's at the Bottom? Examining Claims About Racial Hierarchy." *Ethnic & Racial Studies* 27 (6): 859–877.

Song, Yen Ling. 2007. "China: in the African Firing line." *Energy Compass*, May 25.

Steel Guru. 2011. "Zambia Seeks to Give Job Preference to Nationals Chiefly in Mines to Avoid Exploitation" November 24.

Tesler, Michael. 2012. "The Spillover of Racialization Into Health Care: how President Obama Polarized Public Opinion by Racial Attitudes and Race." *American Journal of Political Science* 56 (3): 690–704.

Thanh Nien News. 2014. "Vietnamese Emigrants Earn Millions in Angola." June 24. www.thanhniennews.com/society/vietnamese-emigrants-make-millions-in-angola-27597.html.

Two Brothers. 2015. "South China Morning Post." January 17.

Versi, Anver. 2014. "Culture clash: Africa's Lukewarm Welcome for the Chinese." *Global: The International Briefing*. www.global-briefing.org/2014/01/culture-clash-africas-lukewarm-welcome-for-the-chinese/.

Wasserman, Herman. 2012. "China in South Africa: Media Responses to a Developing Relationship." *Chinese Journal of Communication* 5 (3): 336–354.

Williams, Craig. 2012. "Submission Regarding Australia's Export Credit Arrangements." March 20. www.pc.gov.au/data/assets/pdf_file/0005/115934/subdr062.pdf.

Wilson, Jake. 2008. "The Racialized Picket Line: White Workers and Racism in the Southern California Supermarket Strike." *Critical Sociology* 34 (3): 349–367.

Windle, Joel. 2008. "The Racialization of African Youth in Australia." *Social Identities* 14 (5): 553–566.

Wong, Hongjuan. 2013. China Luanshya Mine, Zambia, June 25.

Wong, Heung Wah. 1999. *Japanese Bosses, Chinese Workers: Power and Control in a Hong Kong Mega-Store.* London: Curzon.

WorldPublicOpinion.Org. 2008. "Publics Around the World Say Governments Should Act to Prevent Racial Discrimination." www.worldpublicopinion.org/pipa/articles/btjusticehuman_rightsra/460.php.

XXX. Johannesburg, November 19, 2014.

Yan, Hairong. 2014. "Suzhi Travels: Northeast Asia, China, Africa." Presentation, Chinese Agricultural University, Beijing, November 6.

Yang, Lihua. 2002. 理解非洲：我所认识的非洲和非洲人 [Understanding Africa: Africa and Africans in my View], 世界知识. http://iwaas.cass.cn/paper/info.jsp?id=3850.z.

Zhao, Yuling. 2007. Khartoum, December 28.

Zhou, Liang. 2008. Chambishi, August 20.

Zhou, Yuxiao. 2013. Lusaka, July 20.

Zulu, Adam. 2012. Luanshya, August 17.

Socioeconomic attainment, cultural tastes, and ethnic identity: class subjectivities among Uyghurs in Ürümchi

Xiaowei Zang

Department of Applied Social Sciences, City University of Hong Kong, Hong Kong

ABSTRACT

Many scholars have cited socioeconomic status, cultural tastes, and group reference as the major determinants of class identification. Few have conceptualized minority ethnicity as a vital source of class subjectivities, however. I address this knowledge gap in this paper by examining Uyghur subjective class status in Ürümchi, China. I show that income and occupational attainment are not correlated with Uyghur choices of class labels. I also show that Uyghur ethnic identity affects their choices of class labels. I argue that Uyghurs think that they are a dominated group and compare themselves with Han Chinese unfavourably when defining their subjective class positions in Ürümchi. As a result, intergroup competition overshadows the variability in socioeconomic attainments among different Uyghur groups. The implications of these findings for research on class identification in multi-ethnic societies are discussed. Data are drawn from a survey (N = 900) conducted in Ürümchi in 2007.

This paper examines class subjectivities among Uyghurs in Ürümchi in the People's Republic of China (PRC), thereby contributing to research on ethnic relations in Xinjiang and the sociological study of class identity. First, it is necessary to examine how Uyghur ethnic identity has influenced their class identification, which helps our understanding of ethnic conflicts and state-minority relations in Xinjiang. Second, the sociological study of class has not fully examined the effect of minority ethnicity on choices of class labels. This paper draws data from a 2007 survey on Uyghurs (N = 900) in Ürümchi to study how Uyghurs define their class subjectivities and what the main determinants of their class belonging are.

Subjective class status (i.e. class subjectivity, class consciousness, class identification, and class belonging) refers to a person's belief about his or her location in the social hierarchy that reflects his/her cognitive averaging of standard markers of socioeconomic situation (Singh-Manoux, Adler, and Marmot 2003, 1331). I follow Yamaguchi and Wang (2002) in constructing the scale of subjective class status and test effects of cultural tastes and socio-economic status on Uyghur class subjectivities in this paper. I find that socio-economic status is a weak predictor of subjective class status, whereas cultural tastes are closely related to Uyghur class perceptions. I also find that ethnicity matters with regard to Uyghur class belonging. These findings have important implications for research on class identification in multi-ethnic societies. To provide background knowledge for the Ürümchi study, the next section conducts a brief literature review on class subjectivity in the mainstream social sciences.

Existing theories of class identification

Subjective class identities are a key variable in Marxist and Weberian theories that links objective class position to class-based collective action (Davis and Robinson 1998, 1064–1065; Kelley and Evans 1995, 157). Using the Irish in England and various ethno-linguistic groups in the US, Marx and Engels argue that an individual's ethnic identity may confound or undermine his or her class identity (Marx and Engels 1961, xiv, 280–281; Marx and Engels 1971, 292–295).

Influenced by Marx (Evans and Kelley 2004, 3–6; Jackman and Jackman 1973, 570), some scholars have associated socioeconomic factors with subjective class status (Cannot 1984, 123; Crompton 2006, 673; Jackman 1979, 457–458, 460). Hodge and Treiman (1968, 537) show that education, income, and occupation are correlated with class identification in the USA. Jackman (1979, 443) documents the impact of income and occupation on an individual's assessment of his or her subjective class status. Lundberg and Kristenson (2008, 383) and Singh-Manoux, Adler, and Marmot (2003, 1322, 1329, 1331) detect a high degree of congruence between subjective class status and key measures of socioeconomic position (i.e. employment grade, education, and income) in the west. Hunt and Ray (2012) show that education and house-hold income appear more consequential than occupational prestige and self-employment in shaping Blacks' self-reports of their own class positions in the USA. Lindemann (2007, 63–64) finds similar patterns in Estonia. Evans and Kelley (2004, 23–24) report a firm relationship between objective social positions and subject class status in 21 countries.

Socioeconomic status may matter with regard to Uyghur class identification. Rudelson (1997, 117, 119) argues that in pre-1992 Xinjiang, class distinction between intellectuals, merchants, and peasants was clear and strong due to differences in education, income, and occupational prestige. Uyghur 'identity is formed according to social class and occupation rather than family types, descent, or pan-oases solidarity'. The post-1992 era has witnessed a growing Uyghur middle-class and business community (Koch 2006, 15; Roberts 2004, 224; also Mackerras 2005). Rabiye Qadir, the current President of the World Uyghur Congress, was once one of the five richest people in the PRC before she was arrested for her link with Uyghur nationalist activities in 1999. At the same time, as discussed below, many Uyghurs have suffered from discrimination and unemployment. Social stratification may lead different Uyghur groups to perceive their class positions differently.

It is likely that the rich and famous define themselves as upper class, those who are in the middle income category typically consider themselves as middle class, and the poor commonly regard themselves as lower class. It can be argued that Uyghurs are similarly affected by their status attainment (e.g. income and occupation) when thinking of their class belonging. Hence,

Hypothesis 1: Uyghur socioeconomic status is positively related to Uyghur class identification, controlling for other covariates.

An alternative approach towards research on class subjectivities is an emphasis on cultural tastes. For Bourdieu, cultural capital is embodied in people's cultural tastes. Distinction in cultural taste with respect to preferences in clothing, leisure pastimes, music, or reading material can signify social standing and maintain, reinforce, or reproduce existing class hierarchies (Bourdieu 1987, 1993). Drawing upon Bourdieu, Gunn (2005, 49) and Savage and Bennett (2005, 4) argue that class inequality shall be considered not simply as a matter of 'objective' economic inequalities but also as circulating through symbolic and cultural capital. Class is reproduced through among others cultural taste (Skarpenes and Sakslind 2010, 231–232, 236). Cultural taste and symbolic capital that class signifies cannot be reducible to economic factors (Bottero and Irwin 2003, 465; Crompton 2006, 660, 673; Devine 2004, 182; Lawler 2005, 797, 799–800). Skarpenes and Sakslind (2010, 232) and Lawler (2005) recommend a 'culturalist class analysis', broadening the thematic scope of work, family, and economy to include cultural capital (e.g. lifestyle and taste) as objects for sociological enquiry into the formation of class consciousness.

The concept of cultural capital is used in the study of classes in China. Wang, Davis, and Bian (2006) find that volume and composition of cultural capital varies across social classes in urban China. Cultural capital in the form of diversified knowledge and appreciation for certain genres or specific authors is unevenly distributed across social classes, which suggests that the possession of cultural capital is a valuable resource in defining and crystallizing class boundaries in urban China. Those in authority at their workplace (government/party officials and managers) and those with professional or administrative skills not only read highbrow books more often but also read significantly more widely across genres than do other groups.

Presumably, an emphasis on cultural tastes is a valid theory and universally applicable for the study of class subjectivities. Thus, the concept of cultural taste should contribute to understanding how Uyghurs define their class positions. It can be argued that those with more cultural capital consider their class position differently from those with less cultural capital. Hence,

Hypothesis 2: There is a close relationship between cultural capital and class belonging among Uyghurs, everything being the same.

The third approach is reference group theory. Kelley and Evans (1995) argue that people perceive the world as an enlarged version of their reference group. Their subjective images of class reflect a mixture of both materialist forces and the vivid subjective images of equality and consensus among family, friends, and co-workers. These reference group processes distort perceptions of class as individuals assess their class locations in light of educational levels, occupations, and incomes of the people around them. Because family, friends, and co-workers are usually similar, most people see themselves as average and unexceptional. Reference group processes are a special case of the 'availability heuristic', a systematic perceptual bias whereby people base their perceptions on their immediate social milieu, thus overestimating the number of persons similar to themselves, their relatives, and their friends (Kelley and Evans 1995, 158–160; Lindemann 2007, 55; also Evans and Kelley 2004). This may explain why most people in the west consider themselves middle class.

One key reference group is ethnicity: when people compare themselves with others, they use ethnicity as a reference point as much as or more than age, gender, educational attainment, etc. In their study of class consciousness in the USA, Jackman and Jackman (1973, 577–580) claim that the effect of ascriptive ethnic status assumes such overwhelming salience for African-Americans that prestige resulting from achieved statuses takes on relatively minor significance in their self-location in the socioeconomic structure in the USA. Cannot (1984) similarly argues that African-Americans and other ethnic groups perceive class differently. This paper examines whether ethnic identity matters with regard to Uyghur class perceptions.

Uyghurs in Xinjiang

There are 56 officially recognised nationality groups in the PRC. Han Chinese are the ethnic majority group in China, whereas Uyghurs are the fifth largest minority nationality group in China and the ethnic majority in Xinjiang (Zang 2015). According to the sixth PRC census conducted in 2010, Uyghurs in

Xinjiang numbered more than 10 million (46.4%), compared with some 8.4 million (39%) Han Chinese (Australian Centre on China in the World 2012).

The Chinese Communist Party (CCP) took over Xinjiang in 1949 and prosecuted some Uyghurs with 'deviant' political or religious views in the early 1950s (Millward and Tursun 2004, 88–89; Shichor 2005, 127). At the same time, it raised a large group of Uyghur officials, intellectuals, and professionals and recruited many Uyghurs into the state workforce. The vast majority of Uyghurs enjoyed upward mobility and improved their living standards substantially in the 1950s and the 1960s (Benson 2004; also Rudelson 1997; Taynen 2006). This situation was changed during the Cultural Revolution of 1966–1976 (Fuller and Lipman 2004; Van Wie Davis 2008; Hess 2009) as many Uyghur intellectuals and government officials were attacked (Zang 2015).

After the Cultural Revolution, the CCP recognised the damages that had been done to ethnic relations in Xinjiang. To attempt reconciliation, the CCP introduced new policies to open up a relatively tolerant environment for ethnic and religious expression from 1978 to the early 1990s (Rudelson and Jankowiak 2004, 307; Hess 2009, 87). Uyghurs were given some freedom to express their versions of Uyghur history and culture (Rudelson 1997, 115). Pilgrimages to Mecca were resumed in 1979, after a 15-year break (Shichor 2005, 122). The government also accorded Uyghurs a certain level of preferential treatment in the areas of family planning, college admission, job placement, and leadership representation (Rudelson 1997, 125; Koch 2006, 16; Reny 2009, 502).

Hoping to boost ethnic unity and regional stability in Western China, the CCP launched the Great Western Development (西部大开发) campaign in 2000 (Goodman 2004, 317, 319–320). Xinjiang's GDP climbed from 220 billion yuan in 2004 to 352 billion yuan in 2007, 420 billion yuan in 2008, and 657.4 billion yuan in 2011, and its GDP per capita increased from 16,820 yuan in 2007 to 19,798 yuan in 2009 (Xinjiang Demographic Analysis and Economy Overview; Li 2013).

Despite the CCP's efforts to repair ethnic relations in Xinjiang, Uyghur ethnic consciousness has risen steadily since the 1990s. There is an acute sense of separation between Us (Uyghurs) and Them (Han Chinese) (Koch 2006; also Bovingdon 2002; Van Wie Davis 2008). A small number of Uyghur extremists have taken violent action against the Chinese government and Han Chinese (Hess 2009; Shichor 2005; also Zang 2015), whereas the vast majority of Uyghurs have engaged in 'everyday' resistance of a non-violent nature (Rudelson 1997; also Bovingdon 2002).

Uyghur ethnic identity and Uyghur class identity

What has caused rising Uyghur ethnic consciousness since the early 1990s? One possible reason is Han migration to Xinjiang in the post-1978 era. Han migrants are uninterested in learning the Uygur language and 'denigrate the Uyghur language, dress, food, and social customs' (Rudelson 1997, 124; Yee 2005, 42; also Zang 2015). The cultural superiority and general disregard by some Han Chinese towards minority culture may have served to intensify intergroup conflict and strengthen Uyghur identity. In addition, Xinjiang is an autonomous region. There should be major Uyghur representation in the leadership in the government and the ruling CCP, the widespread use of the Uyghur language, etc., in Xinjiang. But in reality, Han Chinese dominate the political and economic systems in the region. The lack of real autonomy has been a major source of Uyghur grievances and ethnic conflict (Cote 2012; Zang 2015).

Equally important, the government policy to intensify market reforms in the post-1992 era (Hou 2011) has promoted economic growth at the expense of equality (Zang 2011, 2012). One report claims that the Gini coefficient in China was around 0.30 in 1980 (which made China one of the most equal countries in the world), but by 2012 it had nearly doubled to 0.55, far surpassing the level of 0.45 in the USA (Xie and Zhou 2014). Another report asserts that the Gini coefficient in China reached 0.73 in 2012 (Zhang 2014). In Xinjiang, inequality has reflected itself in ethnic inequality. Using survey data gathered in Ürümchi in 2005, Zang (2010) shows that 52.3 per cent of the Han respondents work in state firms, as compared with 28.5 per cent of the Uyghur respondents. A job in the state sector is a treasured achievement in Ürümchi. Zang (2011) also finds that Uyghur workers earn 52 per cent less than Han workers in non-state sectors.

Ethnic inequalities have occurred partly because Uyghur–Han differences in schooling, capital, access to bank loans, etc. Unsurprisingly, Han Chinese have been the main beneficiary of government reform policies. The economy in Xinjiang has been 'dominated by Han, not minorities' (Benson 2004, 214; Mackerras 2001, 298–299) and 'Uyghurs are poorer than the Han' (Fuller and Lipman 2004, 325; Toops 2004, 262; also Zang 2015). Ethnic disparity has become an important cleavage that has divided Xinjiang society into two opposite subgroups (i.e. Uyghurs vs. Han Chinese).

The Uyghur–Han division, based on ethnic disparity, has been strengthened by labour market discrimination against Uyghurs. Private Han firms have grown rapidly along with the steady decline of the state sector in the post-1992 era. Because private firms are not legally required to observe affirmative action, Uyghurs have suffered from Han discrimination in the labour market (Amnesty International 1999, 9; Becquelin 2000, 85; Mackerras 2001, 299; also Zang 2011). Many employers in Xinjiang are Han Chinese, who do not think that Uyghur workers are productive and prefer Han workers over Uyghur workers (Becquelin 2000, 85–86; Bovingdon 2002, 45; also Zang 2011). Han discrimination enhances the value of intergroup comparison for Uyghurs in their discourse of their class positions in society. Uyghurs are likely to focus on Uyghur–Han inequalities in their discourse of class subjectivities, which means that they are not likely to highlight variability in status attainment among different Uyghur groups when thinking of their subjective class status. Given the intrinsic relationship between Uyghur ethnic identity and ethnic inequality, the stronger a Uyghur's ethnic identity is, the more likely he or she thinks that Uyghurs are a dominated group in Xinjiang, the less likely he or she considers himself or herself as having good class status. Hence:

Hypothesis 3: Uyghur ethnic identity affects Uyghur subjective class status negatively, holding other covariates constant.

Hypothesis 1 proposes a close link between Uyghur socioeconomic status and Uyghur class identification. In comparison, Hypothesis 3 suggests that Uyghur are not likely to be sensitive to variations resulting from achieved statuses, and it is possible that minority ethnicity is more important than gender, education, and other objective status characteristics in determining Uyghur class subjectivities. However, it is not clear whether the effect of cultural capital on Uyghur class consciousness (i.e. Hypothesis 2) would fade away when status attainment and ethnic identity are controlled for in data analysis.

Data

Ürümchi is the capital of the Xinjiang Uyghur Autonomous Region. It was estimated that Uyghurs represented about 9 per cent of the total population in Ürümchi in 2001 and were not evenly distributed in the city (Zang 2010). Thus, simple random sampling could not used for the 2007 survey. Geographical cluster sampling was used instead. The local collaborators chose 10 neighbourhoods with the highest percentages of Uyghur households in Ürümchi as sampling clusters. However, Badaowan Street and Toutunhe Street, which reported the seventh and tenth highest percentages of Uyghur households in the city, declined to cooperate with the survey takers. Sangong Street, which was ranked the eleventh with 17.06 per cent of Uyghur households among its residents in 2000, was used to make up the shortfall. A total of 1,394 Uyghur households were selected from the nine clusters using probability proportional to size selection methods. Data were collected by face-to-face interviews with one proxy respondent from each household (only those aged between 18 and 65 were selected). Most interviews were conducted in evenings, weekends, or public holidays. Among the sampled 1,394 households, 494 were not interviewed due to unavailability, refusals, or no access to gated residential buildings. In all, the completion rate for the survey was 64.7 per cent ($N = 900$).

Variables and measures

Logistic regression analysis is used to examine the effects of independent variables on the dependent variable (Davis and Robinson 1998, 1069; Yamaguchi and Wang 2002, 447–450). The dependent variable is class identification, which is a dummy variable. Following Jackman (1979, 443, 446) and Yamaguchi and Wang (2002, 451; Also Hodge and Treiman 1968, 536; Jackman and Jackman 1973, 573; Lindemann 2007, 60; Singh-Manoux, Adler, and Marmot 2003, 1322; Skarpenes and Sakslind 2010, 223), in the 2007 survey, the respondents were asked to identify their class membership:

> 'Considering all sorts of socioeconomic indicators such as educational attainment and family income, with which of the following five common social status groups you identify: the upper class, the upper middle class, the middle class, the lower middle class, and the lower class.'

Eight Uyghur respondents (0.9%) defined themselves as upper class, 90 (10%), upper middle class; 420 (46.7%), middle class; 231 (25.8%), lower middle class; and 150 (16.7%), lower class. Following Davis and Robinson (1998, 1068) and Yamaguchi and Wang (2002, 451; also Surridge 2007, 212), the responses are dichotomized to contrast upper, upper middle, and middle classes (= 1) with lower middle and lower classes (= 0).

Independent variables

Data analyses below involve the prediction of subjective class status from a battery of 15 variables. Conceptually, these 15 variables fall into four categories: control variables (age, sex, married status, and religiosity), socioeconomic measures (occupational attainment and income), cultural tastes (education, urban, reading time, and music instruments), and Uyghur ethnic identity.

Control variables. I control for age coded in years (Hunt and Ray 2012, 1470; Wang, Davis, and Bian 2006, 326); gender coded as (1) male and (0) female (Hunt and Ray 2012, 1470; Wang, Davis, and Bian 2006, 326); and marital status coded as (1) married and (0) single, widowed, or divorced (Davis and Robinson 1998, 1069; Hunt and Ray 2012, 1470; Lindemann 2007, 54, 56; Lundberg and Kristenson 2008, 380). I also control religiosity. Zang (2013) discusses in detail how Islam has become part of Uyghur ethnic identity. Thus, religion may affect Uyghur class subjectivities. Stark (1999, 251) points out that the primary concern of research on religiosity 'is with individual piety'. Hence, most scholars have used religious self-identification variables such as religious commitment and activities reported by survey respondents to measure the levels of religiosity (Collett and Lizardo 2009, 213; Miller and Stark 2002, 1409–1410). However, when I constructed the questionnaire for the 2007 survey, I decided not to use mosque attendance since Uyghur women were not allowed to enter the mosque. Thus, in the 2007 survey, the interviewer asked the respondent three questions: (1) 'How often do you pray?' (2) 'How religiously pious do you think you are?' and (3) 'How important is religion in your life?' The frequency of prayers ranges from (1) 'several times a day' to (5) 'once a year or never'. The scale of religious piety ranges from (1) 'very pious' to (5) 'not pious at all'. The importance of religion in life ranges from (1) 'very important' to (5) 'unimportant'. I created a composite index of religiosity by combining the responses to the three items. The Cronbach's alpha is .736, indicating a good degree of reliability or internal consistency. The index ranges from 3 (very religious) to 15 (not very religious).

During the 2007 survey, 16 Uyghur respondents reported no affiliation with the Islamic religion. Thus, I run one regression analysis with the sampled Uyghurs and another with the sampled Uyghurs who are Muslims, which will help us assess whether religiosity affects Uyghur class identity.

Socioeconomic variables. Socioeconomic status is measured by income and occupational attainment (Hunt and Ray 2012, 1470; Singh-Manoux, Adler, and Marmot 2003). Income refers to monthly earnings each respondent received in 2004 and is an interval variable. Next, a measure of occupational attainment is firm ranks. It is an ordinal variable whereby the respondents working in a central or provincial-rank workplace coded as 1, those working in a prefectural or municipal-rank workplace coded as 2, and all others coded as 3. Each workplace in urban China carries an administrative rank from the central government level to the township level. The higher the administrative rank a workplace holds, the more resources it controls, and the more financially affluent its employees are (Bian and Logan 1996).

In addition, four dummy variables are created to measure occupational attainment: professional (= 1), office worker (= 1), *getihu* (= 1), and fulltime work (= 1) (Wang, Davis, and Bian 2006, 326; also see Junisbai 2010, 1687; Lindemann 2007, 54, 58, 60; Lundberg and Kristenson 2008, 378–379; Singh-Manoux, Adler, and Marmot 2003, 1323; Yamaguchi and Wang 2002, 451). Professionals include accountants, engineers, doctors, etc. Office workers refer to executive assistants, clerks, etc. *Getihu* are small entrepreneurs, shop owners, etc. Fulltime work is a dummy variable with fulltime workers coded as 1 and others as 0.

Cultural tastes. Measures of cultural tastes include education, urban status, newspaper reading time, and ownership of music instruments. Although education is often regarded as an indicator of socioeconomic achievements, some scholars consider it as a vital measure of cultural capital. Culture is transmitted though formal education, which is a key to the reproduction of classes (Skarpenes and Sakslind 2010, 231–232, 236; Wang, Davis, and Bian 2006, 320). Education is in six ordered categories ranging from (1) no formal education to (6) university-level education.

Urban status is a dummy variable with residents with urban hukou coded as 1 and rural migrants coded as 0. People in China are governed by a household registration system that arbitrarily and unjustifiably divides people into urban hukou and rural hukou with different entitlements and life chances (Chan 2009). Urban people in China are perceived to be more educated, civilized and cultured than rural farmers. Urban Uyghurs similarly think that they are more cultural than their rural cousins (Rudelson 1997). Reading is considered as an indicator of cultural participation and taste and hence of social class membership (Le Roux et al. 2008; Prieur and Savage 2011). Newspaper reading is similarly seen as part of the activities by middle class people in China, who are generally regarded as 'educated persons' and 'cultured persons'. Newspaper reading time refers to the total amount of time each respondent devoted to reading newspapers and is a continuous variable (Wang, Davis, and Bian 2006, 318, 321–322). Finally, music is commonly esteemed as part of highbrow culture and a form of class distinction (Katz-Gerro 1999; Prieur and Savage 2011; Purhonen, Gronow, and Rahkonen 2011). The ownership of music instruments at home is a dummy variable with the respondents who owned music instruments coded as 1 and others as 0.

Uyghur identity. In the 2007 survey, two questionnaire items were used to solicit information on Uyghur ethnic identity. Each of the two items is coded from 1 (very important) to 10 (not very important), with lower scores indicating higher levels of Uyghur ethnic identity. The first item reads: 'It is vital for Uyghurs to use Uyghur language'. Xinjiang's economy is dominated by Han Chinese. Some Uyghurs have been 'lured by new opportunities in education, employment and trade' in the Han-dominated sectors (Benson 2004, 213; Fuller and Lipman 2004, 323–324). They have looked on knowledge of Chinese language 'as the sine qua non for secular advancement' (Becquelin 2004, 376; Benson 2004, 198–199, 213–214; Fuller and Lipman 2004, 334–335; also Taynen 2006). Thus, those who insist on the importance of speaking Uyghur are likely to have a high level of ethnic identity.

The second item reads: 'It is vital for Uyghurs to promote Uyghur culture'. It is noted that some Uyghurs 'have been assimilated into Chinese society – mastered the Chinese language, achieved public recognition, and become professionals, officials, intellectuals, or celebrities ... ' Some Uyghurs have embraced 'a secular Sinocentrism' at the expense of Uyghur identity (Rudelson and Jankowiak 2004, 310–311, 313–314). They are unlikely to consider it vital to promote Uyghur culture. In addition, the Chinese Government is hostile to attempts by Uyghurs to promote their identity and culture. Under this environment, those who explicitly insist on the promotion of Uyghur culture are likely to have a high level of ethnic identity.

I recoded the responses from 10 scales to 5 scales because many respondents thought it was vital to speak Uyghur and promote Uyghur culture. I then created a composite index of Uyghur identity by combining the responses to these two items. The Cronbach's alpha is .838, indicating a high degree of reliability or internal consistency. The index ranges from 2 (very important) to 10 (not very important).

Findings

Table 1 reports the key background characteristics of the Uyghur respondents. It can be seen that the average age of the respondents is nearly 39 years old, 47.7 per cent of them are men, 65.7 per cent of them are married, and nearly 90 per cent of them are urban residents. In terms of occupational attainment, 53.8 per cent of the Uyghur respondents have a fulltime job, 5.3 per cent of them are office workers, 11.8 per cent are professionals, and 14.1 per cent are *getihu*. Also, 19.2 per cent of the Uyghur respondents work in a central or provincial level workplace, and 20.8 per cent of them work in a prefectural or municipal workplace.

In addition, the distribution of income and that of reading time among Uyghurs are highly skewed. They are log-transformed to establish normality and constant error variance to obtain better linearity in the regression function in Table 3. Also, the mean of Uyghur ethnic identity is 3.04. Recall that the index ranges from 2 (very important) to 10 (not very important), making the midpoint at 4.5. It can be said that Uyghurs hold strong ethnic identity. Finally, Table 1 reports that 57.6 per cent of the Uyghur respondents thought they were middle class.

Table 1. Key background characteristics.

Descriptive statistics	% or mean/SD	N
Controls		
Age (mean/SD)	38.60/12.98	900
Men (%)	47.7%	427
Married (%)	65.7%	591
Religiosity (mean/SD)	7.93/3.02	884
Socioeconomic attainment		
Fulltime work (%)	53.8%	484
Firm rank (%)		
Central and provincial	19.2%	173
Prefectural/municipal	20.8%	187
Street and below	60.0%	540
Income (mean/SD)	833.86/956.23	900
Office worker (%)	5.3%	48
Professional (%)	11.8%	106
Getihu (%)	14.1%	127
Cultural tastes		
Urban status (%)	89.8%	808
Education (%)		
Illiterate/semi-illiterate	5.1%	46
Primary school	16.7%	150
Junior high school	24.4%	220
Senior high school	16.6%	149
Vocational school	10.0%	90
University	27.2%	245
Reading time (mean/SD)	24.7/37.94	900
Music instrument (%)	32.4%	292
Uyghur identity (mean/SD)	3.04/1.80	900
Middle class (%)	57.6%	518

Table 2 shows the correlations between class belonging and covariates among the Uyghur respondents and Uygur Muslims respectively. It can be seen that all measures of socioeconomic attainment are statistically correlated with Uyghur class perceptions, tentatively supporting Hypothesis 1. For example, both office workers and professionals consider themselves as middle class, whereas *getihu* are not likely to do so. Firm ranks are negatively related to the dependent variable, i.e. Uyghur workers employed in high rank workplaces are more likely than others to think that they are middle class. Consistent with Hypothesis 2, the key measures of cultural tastes are associated with the choice of the middle class over that of the lower class by the Uyghur respondents. Finally, Table 2 shows the close correlation between Uyghur ethnic identity and identification with the middle class, tentatively supporting Hypothesis 3 that ethnic identity matters in defining class status by Uyghurs.

The above findings are derived from bivariate analyses. It is not clear if these findings are the outcomes of spurious relationships. Thus, two logistic regression analyses were performed to examine the relationship between the dependent and independent variables. Model 1 of Table 3 shows the clear effect of cultural tastes on the choices of class labels by Uyghurs in Ürümchi. Uyghurs with more cultural or symbolic capital are more likely than others to consider themselves middle class. For example, better educated Uyghurs are more likely than poorly educated Uyghurs to rate themselves high in the class status hierarchy.

The findings from model 1 of Table 3 evidently do not support Hypothesis 1: most socioeconomic variables do not have a statistically significant impact

Table 2. Correlations with higher class identification.

Covariates	Ürümchi sample	Uyghur Muslims
Age	.000 (.996)	.003 (.929)
Male	.037 (.266)	.034 (.317)
Married	.075 (.024)*	.074 (.028)*
Fulltime work	.106 (.002)**	.104 (.002)**
Firm rank	−.208 (.000)***	−.203 (.000)***
Income	.105 (.002)**	.105 (.002)**
Office worker	.094 (.005)**	.100 (.003)**
Professional	.181 (.000)***	.184 (.000)***
Getihu	−.104 (.002)**	−.101 (.003)**
Urban	.193 (.000)***	.191 (.000)***
Education	.369 (.000)***	.364 (.000)***
Reading time	.192 (.000)***	.188 (.000)***
Music instrument	.182 (.000)***	.188 (.000)***
Uyghur identity	.073 (.029)*	.071 (.034)*
Religiosity	–	.139 (.000)***
N	900	884

Note: Figures in parentheses are the sig. (two-tailed) values.
*$p < .05$.
**$p < .01$.
***$p < .001$.

Table 3. Logistic regression analyses of Uyghur class identification.

Covariates	Model 1 Ürümchi sample	Model 2 Uyghur Muslims
Controls		
Age	.003 (.007)	.005 (.008)
Male	.035 (.162)	.018 (.165)
Married	.360 (.179)*	.364 (.179)*
Religiosity	–	.134 (.191)
Socioeconomic attainment		
Fulltime work	.157 (.224)	.173 (.226)
Firm rank	−.316 (.132)*	−.276 (.134)*
Income	−.049 (.041)	−.047 (.041)
Office worker	.043 (.394)	.174 (.408)
Professional	.335 (.314)	.384 (.321)
Getihu	.159 (.263)	.150 (.264)
Cultural tastes		
Urban	.715 (.272)**	.699 (.272)**
Education	.379 (.062)***	.367 (.062)***
Reading time	.178 (.049)***	.172 (.050)***
Music instrument	.470 (.169)**	.485 (.171)**
Uyghur identity	.099 (.045)*	.092 (.046)*
Chi-square	189.021***	183.032***
df	14	15
−2 log likelihood	1,038.014	1,024.432
N	900	884

Note: Figures in parentheses are standard errors.
*$p < .05$.
**$p < .01$.
***$p < .001$.

on the dependent variable. The exception is the coefficient for Firm ranks. This is probably because all high administrative rank workplaces in Xinjiang are government agencies, the offices of the CCP, or large state companies such as Sinopec and China Telecom that employ highly educated workers. Additional analyses show that educations and professional occupations are statistically related to the probabilities of working in highly ranked workplace. These findings, when combined with the above finding about cultural tastes and class perceptions, suggest that Uyghurs are likely to favour a culturalist class analysis over a materialist approach in their discourse of class status. Indeed, it can be seen form model 1 of Table 3 that the measures of cultural tastes are statistically related to Uyghur class consciousness, everything being the same. These findings support Hypothesis 2 unequivocally. Finally, the findings from model 1 of Table 3 support Hypothesis 3 unambiguously as the choices of class labels for oneself are influenced by Uyghur identity, controlling for demographics, socioeconomic status, and cultural tastes in the equation. Uyghurs with high levels of ethnic identity tend not to identify themselves as the upper middle class or the middle class and vice versa.

It is necessary to point out that religiosity is not controlled for in model 1 of Table 3 because 16 Uyghur respondents are not Muslims. They are excluded from analysis in model 2 of Table 3. It can be seen that the inclusion of religiosity in the equation does not lead to major changes in the patterns reported in model 1 of Table 3.

Summary and discussion

Beginning with Centers' work on the psychology of social classes (1949), there has been research on class self-placements. However, many studies have focused on how people in developed countries perceive their class positions. Few have examined class perceptions in less developed countries. In addition, there have been few attempts to conceptualize and test the impact of minority ethnicity on the formation of class subjectivity (Jackman 1979, 459; Jackman and Jackman 1973, 572; Yamaguchi and Wang 2002, 453; also Kluegel and Smith 1981; Lindemann 2007; Lundberg and Kristenson 2008). When a scholar includes ethnicity in research on class perceptions, his or her main focus is on the choices of class labels by the general population, women, or the ethnic majority group (e.g. Crompton 2006; Lawler 2005). The exception is Evans and Kelley's study of subjective social positions in 21 countries including the Philippines (2004).

This paper contributes to this literature with a focus on China. Also, it maps the contours and main determinants of class consciousness among Uyghurs, a dominated ethnic minority group in Xinjiang, China. It also shows the effect of cultural tastes on Uyghur class belonging. As noted, some existing studies have maintained that cultural capital matters with regard to the choices of class labels. Much of research on cultural tastes and class subjectivities are qualitative studies. This paper establishes an empirical link between cultural capital and Uyghur class identification, holding other independent variable constant.

Equally important, some existing studies have found the relationship between objective socioeconomic status and subjective class status. However, this paper shows that Uyghur class perceptions are not related to income and occupational attainment, controlling for main background characteristics. It is plausible that Han dominance in politics and the economy and Han discriminatory attitudes and practices have dictated the ways Uyghurs have perceived their class positions, so much as that intergroup comparisons have overshadowed the variability in socioeconomic attainments in the Uyghur discourse of subjective class status. The attachment to ethnic identity is of such overwhelming salience to Uyghurs that status achievements such as income and occupations do not make a substantive impact on their class identification, as they tend to compare their life chances with those of Han Chinese rather than with those of their compatriots. Heightened Uyghur ethnic identity is a more salient issue than gender, schooling, etc., in the public consciousness and discourse of social hierarchies in society. It is likely that social class has been experienced by

Uyghurs as an ethnic affinity as much as a cultural process or an objective, economic affinity, and that social class has been 'lived' in ethnic ways in Xinjiang.

While this account partly explains the relationship among status attainment, ethnic identity, and class belonging among Uyghurs, it may also partly explain the close link between socioeconomic hierarchies and subjective class status among whites in Estonia (Lindemann 2007), Sweden (Lundberg and Kristenson 2008), the USA (Hodge and Treiman 1968; Jackman 1979), and the UK (Crompton 2006; Singh-Manoux, Adler, and Marmot 2003) since they are not subject to racial discrimination. Thus, intra-group variability in socioeconomic attainments becomes a major determinant of their choices of class labels. In a sense, these findings and the findings from this paper complement and strengthen each other. Furthermore, it can be argued that the ethnic majority and ethnic minorities use different criteria in defining subjective class status because of their different socioeconomic positions and exposure to discrimination in society.

Of course, the findings presented in this paper shall be read with caution since Ürümchi is the capital of Xinjiang and is not representative of the rest of Xinjiang, given the heavy concentration of Uyghur intellectuals and professionals in the city. In addition, Ürümchi has a large Han population whereas many Uyghur migrants are from Southern Xinjiang where there are fewer Han Chinese. Given the reference group theory mentioned above, the preponderance of Han Chinese in Urumqi is likely to influence Uyghurs' class identification. This may partly explain why Uyghur-Han competition overshadows intra-group variability in socioeconomic attainments among Uyghurs.

In sum, this paper highlights ethnic identity as a main determinant of class self-placements. It argues that minority ethnicity is intrinsically related to cultural tastes. It is a key reference point for social comparisons in multi-ethnic society. As discussed above, Uyghur ethnic identity carries with it a sense of 'class opposition' between 'them' (the dominant group, Han Chinese) and 'us' (the dominated group, Uyghurs). Moreover, since Uyghurs think they are dominated group in Xinjiang, they are likely to consider themselves members of the lower class. It is likely that some other ethnic minorities (perhaps not so for Mongols and Koreans) in China and those in other societies feel the same way when they think of their subjective class status. Thus, future research shall include ethnic identity in the study of class identification in multi-ethnic societies.

Disclosure statement

No potential conflict of interest was reported by the authors.

References

Amnesty International. 1999. "China: Gross Violations of Human Rights in the Xinjiang Uighur Autonomous Region." Accessed March 3, 2015. http://www.amnesty.org/en/library/binfo/ ASA17/018/1999.

Australian Centre on China in the World. 2012. "Xinjiang 新疆." Accessed November 8, 2014 http://www.thechinastory.org/lexicon/xinjiang/.

Becquelin, Nicolas. 2000. "Xinjiang in the Nineties." *The China Journal* 44: 65–90.

Becquelin, Nicolas. 2004. "Staged Development in Xinjiang." *The China Quarterly* 178: 358–378.

Benson, Linda. 2004. "Education and Social Mobility among Minority Populations." In *Xinjiang: China's Muslim Borderland*, edited by S. Frederick Starr, 190–215. Armonk: M.E. Sharpe.

Bian, Yanjie, and, John Logan. 1996. "Market Transition and Income Inequality in Urban China." *American Sociological Review* 61 (5): 739–758.

Bottero, Wendy, and Sarah Irwin. 2003. "Locating Difference: Class, 'Race', and Gender, and the Shaping of Social Inequalities." *The Sociological Review* 51 (4): 463–483.

Bourdieu, Pierre. 1987. *Distinction: A Social Critique of the Judgment of Taste.* Translated by Richard Nice. Cambridge: Harvard University Press.

Bourdieu, Pierre. 1993. "The Market of Symbolic Goods." In *The Field of Cultural Production: Essays on Art and Literature*, edited by Randal Johnson, 112–41. New York: Columbia University Press.

Bovingdon, Gardner. 2002. "The Not-So-Silent Majority: Uyghur Resistance to Han Rule in Xinjiang." *Modern China* 28 (1): 39–78.

Cannot, Lynn Weber. 1984. "Trends in Class Identification among Black Americans from 1952 to 1978." *Social Science Quarterly* 65 (1): 112–126.

Centers, Richard. 1949. *The Psychology of Social Classes.* Princeton, NJ: Princeton University Press.

Chan, Kam Wing. 2009. "The Chinese Hukou System at 50." *Eurasian Geography and Economics* 50 (2): 197–221.

Collett, Jessica and Omar Lizardo. 2009. "A Power-Control Theory of Gender and Religiosity." *Journal for the Scientific Study of Religion* 48 (2): 213–231.

Cote, Isabelle. 2012. "Autonomy and Ethnic Diversity." In *Political Autonomy and Divided Societies*, edited by Alain G. Gagnon and Michael Keating, 171–84. London: Palgrave Macmillan.

Crompton, Rosemary. 2006. "Class and Family." *The Sociological Review* 54 (4): 658–677.

Davis, Nancy, and Robert Robinson. 1998. "Do Wives Matter: Class Identities of Wives and Husbands in the United States." *Social Forces* 76 (3): 1063–1086.

Devine, Fiona. 2004. *Class Practices.* Cambridge: Cambridge University Press.

Evans, M. D. R., and Jonathan Kelley. 2004. "Subjective Social Location." *International Journal of Public Opinion Research* 16 (1): 3–38.

Fuller, Graham, and Jonathan Lipman. 2004. "Islam in Xinjiang." In *Xinjiang*, edited by S. Frederick Starr, 320–347. Armonk: M.E. Sharpe.

Goodman, David. 2004. "The Campaign to 'Open up the West'." *China Quarterly* 178: 318–334.

Gunn, Simon. 2005. "Translating Bourdieu: Cultural Capital and the English Middle Class in Historical Perspective." *British Journal of Sociology* 56 (1): 49–64.

Hess, Stephen E. 2009. *Islam, Local Elites, and China's Missteps in Integrating the Uyghur Nation* (pp. 75–96). Accessed March 2, 2015. http://www.usak.org.tr/dosyalar/dergi/4EeTmxtDNppkrrFTak6s43XcfD6iHq.pdf.

Hodge, Robert W., and Donald Treiman. 1968. "Class Identification in the United States." *American Journal of Sociology* 73 (5): 535–547.

Hou, Jack W. 2011. "Economic Reform of China: Cause and Effects." *Social Science Journal* 48 (3): 419–434.

Hunt, Matthew, and Rashawn Ray. 2012. "Social Class Identification among Black Americans." *American Behavioral Scientist* 56 (11): 1462–1480.

Jackman, Mary. 1979. "The Subjective Meaning of Social Class Identification in the United States." *Public Opinion Quarterly* 43 (4): 443–462.

Jackman, Mary, and Robert Jackman. 1973. "An Interpretation of the Relation Between Objective and Subjective Social Status." *American Sociological Review* 38 (5): 569–582.

Junisbai, Azamat. 2010. "Understanding Economic Justice Attitudes in Two (formerly similar) Countries: Kazakhstan and Kyrgyzstan." *Social Forces* 88 (4): 1677–1702.

Katz-Gerro, Tally. 1999. "Cultural Consumption and Social Stratification: Leisure Activities, Musical Tastes, and Social Location." *Sociological Perspectives* 42 (4): 627–646.

Kelley, Jonathan, and M. D. R. Evans. 1995. "Class and Class Conflict in six Western Nations." *American Sociological Review* 60 (2): 157–178.

Kluegel, James, and Smith Eliot. 1981. "Beliefs About Stratification." *Annual Review of Sociology* 7: 29–56.

Koch, Jessica. 2006. "Economic Development and Ethnic Separatism in Western China." Accessed November 11, 2014. http://wwwarc.murdoch.edu.au/publications/wp/wp134.pdf.

Lawler, Stephanie. 2005. "Introduction: Class, Culture and Identity." *Sociology* 39 (5): 797–806.

Le Roux, Rrigitte, Henry Rouanet, Mike Savage, and Alan Warde. 2008. "Class and Cultural Division in the UK." *Sociology* 42 (6): 1049–1071.

Li, Xiaoxia (李晓霞). 2013. "How to Maintain Stability with Rapid Economic Development in Xinjiang [新疆跨越式发展下如何实现长治久安]." Accessed March 3, 2015. http://blog.ifeng.com/article/22186096.html.

Lindemann, Kristina. 2007. "The Impact of Objective Characteristics on Subjective Social Position." *Trames* 11 (1): 54–68.

Lundberg, Johanna, and Margareta Kristenson. 2008. "Is Subjective Status Influenced by Psychosocial Factors?" *Social Indicators Research* 89 (3): 375–390.

Mackerras, Colin. 2001. "Xinjiang at the Turn of the Century." *Central Asian Survey* 20 (3): 289–303.

Mackerras, Colin. 2005. "China's Ethnic Minorities and the Middle Classes." *International Journal of Social Economics* 32 (9): 814–826.

Marx, Karl, and Frederick Engels. 1961. *The Civil War in the United States*. New York: International Publishers.

Marx, Karl, and Frederick Engels. 1971. *On Ireland*. London: Lawrence and Wishart.

Miller, Alan, and Rodney Stark. 2002. "Gender and Religiousness." *American Journal of Sociology* 107 (6): 1399–1423.

Millward, James, and Nabijan Tursun. 2004. "Political History and Strategies of Control, 1884–1978." In *Xinjiang*, edited by S. Frederick Starr, 63–98. Armonk: M.E. Sharpe.

Prieur, Annick and Mike Savage. 2011. "Updating Cultural Capital Theory." *Poetics* 39 (6): 566–580.

Purhonen, Semi, Jukka Gronow, and Keijo Rahkonen. 2011. "Highbrow Culture in Finland." *Acta Sociologica* 54 (4): 385–402.

Reny, Marie-Eve. 2009. "The Political Salience of Language and Religion." *Ethnic and Racial Studies* 32 (3): 490–521.

Roberts, Sean. 2004. "A Land of Borderlands." In *Xinjiang: China's Muslim Borderland*, edited by S. Frederick Starr, 216–37. Armonk: M.E. Sharpe.

Rudelson, Justin. 1997. *Oasis Identities*. New York: Columbia University Press.

Rudelson, Justin, and William Jankowiak. 2004. "Acculturation and Resistance." In *Xinjiang*, edited by S. Frederick Starr, 299–319. Armonk: M.E. Sharpe.

Savage, Mike and Tony Bennett. 2005. "Editors' Introduction: Cultural Capital and Social Inequality." *The British Journal of Sociology* 56 (1): 1–12.

Singh-Manoux, Archana, Nancy Adler, and Michael Marmot. 2003. "Subjective Social Status." *Social Science & Medicine* 56 (6): 1321–1333.

Shichor, Yitzhak. 2005. "Blow Up." *Asian Affairs: An American Review* 32 (2): 119–136.

Skarpenes, Ove and Rune Sakslind. 2010. "Education and Egalitarianism: The Culture of the Norwegian Middle Class." *The Sociological Review* 58 (2): 219–243.

Stark, Rodney. 1999. "Secularization, R.I.P." *Sociology of Education* 60 (3): 249–273.

Surridge, Paul. 2007. "Class Belonging: A Quantitative Exploration of Identity and Consciousness." *The British Journal of Sociology* 58 (2): 207–226.

Taynen, Jennifer. 2006. "Interpreters, Arbiters or Outsiders." *Journal of Muslim Minority Affairs* 26 (1): 45–62.

Toops, Stanley W. 2004. "The Demography of Xinjiang." In *Xinjiang: China's Muslim Borderland*, edited by S. Frederick Star, 241–265. Armonk: M.E. Sharpe.

Van Wie Davis, Elizabeth. 2008. "Uyghur Muslim Ethnic Separatism in Xinjiang, China." *Asian Affairs: An American Review* 35 (1): 15–30.

Wang, Shaoguang, Deborah Davis, and Yanjie Bian. 2006. "The Uneven Distribution of Cultural Capital: Book Reading in Urban China." *Modern China* 32 (3): 315–348.

Xie, Yu, and Xiang Zhou. 2014. "Income Inequality in Today's China." *Proceedings of the National Academy of Sciences of the United States of America* 111 (19): 6928–6933.

Yamaguchi, Kazuo, and Yanto Wang. 2002. "Class Identification of Married Employed Women and men in America." *American Journal of Sociology* 108 (2): 440–475.

Yee, Herbert. 2005. "Ethnic Consciousness and Identity." *Asian Ethnicity* 6 (1): 35–50.

Zang, Xiaowei. 2010. "Affirmative Action, Economic Reforms, and Han-Uyghur Variation in job Attainment in the State Sector in Ürümchi." *The China Quarterly* 202: 344–361.

Zang, Xiaowei. 2011. "Uyghur-Han Earnings Differentials in Ürümchi." *China Journal* 65: 141–155.

Zang, Xiaowei. 2012. "Age and the Cost of Being Uyghurs in Urümchi." *China Quarterly* 210: 419–434.

Zang, Xiaowei. 2013. "Major Determinants of Uyghur Ethnic Consciousness in Urümchi." *Modern Asian Studies* 47 (6): 2046–2071.

Zang, Xiaowei. 2015. *Ethnicity in China: A Critical Introduction*. Cambridge: Polity Press.

Zhang, Xinyi (张心怡). 2014. "Beijing University Release the 2014 Report on Living Standards in China 2014 [北京大学发布《中国民生发展报告· 2014》]." Accessed March 3, 2015. http://news.sciencenet.cn/htmlnews/2014/8/300472.shtm.

Blurring boundaries and negotiating subjectivities – the Uyghurized Han of southern Xinjiang, China

Agnieszka Joniak-Lüthi

Department of Social and Cultural Anthropology, LMU Munich, Munich, Germany

ABSTRACT

Negotiations of collective subjectivities among the Han living in ethnic minority areas of the People's Republic of China have so far received little attention. This article explores one such process among the 'Uyghurized Han' living in southern Xinjiang Uyghur Autonomous Region, an area in which Han make up less than one-fourth of the population. Based on research material collected during long-term ethnographic fieldwork, this article suggests that Uyghurized Han creatively construct a sense of belonging in Xinjiang by positioning themselves at the interface of Han-ness and Uyghur-ness. They do so by engaging in contradictory but nonetheless simultaneous processes of blurring and fixing boundaries of identity vis-à-vis both Uyghur and other Han. The aim of the present article is to discuss the ways in which their collective subjectivities are produced in the process of boundary negotiation.

In authoritarian multi-ethnic countries like the People's Republic of China and the former Soviet Union, the Han Chinese and Russians respectively, have been constructed as 'majority nationalities'. In official discourse these 'majorities' have been represented as culturally advanced and 'politically awake', and as the agents of development and modernization. They have been necessarily constructed in this way in relation to the 'minority national-ities', which are represented as their exact opposite: backward, powerless, and undeveloped (Gladney 1994). Members of national majorities rarely face the necessity, or feel the urge, to re-negotiate this relationship as it is officially sanctioned by the state. Even when they settle in those regions of their home countries which are numerically dominated by the minorities, the set-tlers attempt to impose their officially privileged position onto these settings as well. While this is the prevailing pattern, my research in southern Xinjiang

Uyghur Autonomous Region in northwest China (Figure 1) suggests that other social dynamics also exist. The present article explores some identity positions that come into being when Han – China's 'majority nationality' – encounter Uyghur, the majority group in Xinjiang and one of the most significant 'others' for the Han in general (Chu, n.d.).

Furthermore, the present article engages in the debate on the relationship between ethnicity and *minzu* in China. *Minzu*, the Chinese counterpart of the Soviet 'nationality', are officially recognized population categories. Fifty-six *minzu* were recognized following the Minzu Classification (Minzu Shibie) – a major social-engineering project launched in the early 1950s by the Chinese Communist government. The result of the project was a division of the Chinese population into the Han majority *minzu* and 55 minority *minzu* (*shaoshu minzu*) (Fei 1980; Gladney 1998; Mullaney 2011). As the number of *minzu* had to be limited to enable their effective administrative management, often a number of locally significant ethnic varieties were incorporated into one *minzu*. *Minzu* are thus different from ethnic groups as they were created by the state according to a specific political agenda. Nevertheless, the research material discussed here suggests that there are also important parallels between *minzu* and ethnicity as collective subjectivities today, 60 years after the project. The present article discusses these parallels, as well as differences, and shows how the study of Chinese *minzu* can contribute to ethnicity studies in general.

In the anthropology of China, boundary negotiations, intra-*minzu* differentiation, trans-*minzu* alliances, and other mundane identity processes of the Han living in China's multiethnic regions remain understudied.[1] While a significant body of research on identity processes among China's ethnic

Figure 1. Xinjiang's location (source: http://edition.cnn.com/).

minorities has emerged in the West since the late 1990s, similar processes among the Han have received far less attention. This paucity of research deprives our understanding of Han-ness of its pluralistic and transient formulations and enactments, and its interpenetrations with other collective subjectivities. Furthermore, it does not allow for questioning – and thus facilitates circulation of – monolithic representations of 'the Han' constructed during the various Han making projects. The lack of research also veils the 'collisions' between state-promoted identity hierarchies and other processes of identity formation. In Xinjiang, the paucity of research on multiple and changing Han subjectivities makes them appear as a homogeneous category of identity. The aim of this article is to take apart this category by focusing on Uyghurized Han in southern Xinjiang, that is, Han who through long-term residence in the region have assumed markers of Uyghurness. The article analyses the way in which Uyghurized Han negotiate the boundaries of their identity vis-à-vis the Uyghur and vis-à-vis other Han. It also explores the ways in which Uyghurized Han cultivate a sense of attachment to a region where Han presence is a contested issue.

Fieldwork

I collected the research material discussed here during twelve months of anthropological fieldwork in Xinjiang between 2011 and 2015. Most of this time I spent in Aqsu District in southern Xinjiang; I also travelled extensively in the area encompassed by three oasis towns of Aqsu, Kashgar and Hotan.[2] Moreover, I conducted three and a half months of the fieldwork in Ürümchi, the regional capital. Long-term, anthropological fieldwork in southern Xinjiang is today difficult to conduct. Suspicion of local authorities towards foreigners is extremely high, as is the fear that these foreigners might be negatively affected by the increasing violence in the region. In my case, without extensive social networks and energetic assistance of my local research partners, it would have been impossible to conduct fieldwork in Aqsu and live with Uyghur families there and in Ürümchi. These families' good reputation and extensive social networks protected not only themselves from the negative repercussions of my presence, but also probably shielded me from harassment by the authorities.

Though I lived with Uyghur families, I also socialized with Han on a daily basis. This paper is based on around 60 semi-structured interviews with both Han and Uyghur individuals, and on the material collected through participant observation. Most of the interviews were conducted in standard Chinese. Some of them were in English and German when my interviewees themselves felt more comfortable using these languages to communicate with a foreigner. Some conversations were also conducted in Uyghur; in that case a third person interpreted into English or German as my Uyghur was only sufficient for basic conversations. When it makes sense, as in cases when certain processes involve the broader region, I complement my material from Aqsu with references to other locations. In all cases, names of the research participants have been altered and the locations of places are indicated only approximately.

The county town of Aqsu has a large population of post-1949 Han settlers and migrants who constitute about 60 per cent of a population of 291,000 in the urban area The Uyghur comprise the remaining 40 per cent. At the same time, in Aqsu District – which includes both urban and rural areas – the Han constitute a clear numerical minority (Figure 2).

Aqsu, like almost all of southern Xinjiang and Ürümchi, has been affected by the apparently increasing intra-*minzu* (Uyghur-Uyghur) and inter-*minzu* (Uyghur-Han) violence. While in 2011–2012 this violence was referred to by only some of my research participants, in 2015 the majority of my Han interlocutors commented on the increasing sense of insecurity. It is said that large numbers of Han are leaving southern Xinjiang in fear of their lives. The present article has thus to be read against a backdrop of the increasing mobilization of Han and Uyghur *minzu* labels in the aftermath of the 2009 Ürümchi riot, the attack in the Kunming railway station, and the bomb attack in a market street in Ürümchi in 2014 – to mention just those incidents extensively reported by the Western media. The Han I focus on in this article are not untouched by this mobilization of identity labels. In some cases they report a growing distance in their relationships with Uyghur. Some Uyghurized Han also prefer to downplay the 'Uyghurized' elements of their identity vis-à-vis other Han for fear of social exclusion.

Han and Uyghur in Xinjiang

In 1949, when the People's Republic of China was founded, Xinjiang was an overwhelmingly Muslim region with a large population of Uyghur, Kazakh, Kyrgyz, and Dungan (Hui), among others, who were also found across the border in the Soviet Union. The Uyghur, still the region's largest *minzu*

	1953	1964	1982	1990	2000	2010
Han population in Aqsu District	4,300	164,900	329,800	333,500	570,147 (Incl. Aral)	685,267 (Incl. Aral)
Share in district population	0.5%	17.3%	21.9%	19.4%	26.6%	27%

Figure 2. Han population in Aqsu District (based on Akesu Diqu Tongjiju (2011), Li (2010, 67) and Toops (2013, 19–21)).

speak a Turkic language. The Uyghur language and Uzbek, Kazak, Kyrgyz and even modern Turkish are mutually intelligible to a certain extent. Uyghur and standard Chinese, on the other hand, are mutually intelligible. Religious, linguistic and cultural continuities link Xinjiang to Central Asia and the international Islamic *Umma*. These continuities pose a significant challenge to the Chinese government as it tries to integrate the region into the Chinese nation-state. The Uyghur in particular contest the Chinese administration of their homeland, the ways in which the region is being 'developed', and Han immigration.

Although some Han/Chinese[3] traders, administrators and soldiers lived in Xinjiang before 1949, they only made up about 6 per cent of the population at the time of the first local census (XWZCZ 2005, 205). Since then, large-scale Han settlement in Xinjiang has been promoted by the state. Construction of transportation networks, extensive irrigated agriculture, industrialization, construction of new towns and settlements all required man-power and settlers for their long-term maintenance. As a result, the Han population has grown from 291,021 in 1949 to 8.8 million in 2010. This makes the Han into the second largest *minzu* in the region today after the Uyghur, whose population has grown from 3.2 million in 1949 to slightly more than 10 million in 2010.[4]

The accuracy of the Han population numbers in the 2010 census can be disputed due to the fact that the census omitted army personnel. In addition, because the census was conducted on November 1, seasonal workers who reside in Xinjiang between March and late October were omitted as well. More importantly for this paper, however, the census demonstrates that there are huge regional differences in terms of the distribution of Han and Uyghur in Xinjiang (Figures 3 and 4).

In northern Xinjiang, the Han are clearly in the majority. In southern Xinjiang, especially in the three districts of Aqsu, Kashgar and Hotan, the Han are a clear minority. While there are significant Han communities in each of these three district towns, the majority of smaller towns and the countryside are Uyghur-dominated spaces. Due to the current expansion of jujube and walnut plantations in southern Xinjiang, the number of Han employed in agriculture and those who cater to them is growing. This is, however, a fairly recent phenomenon and the majority of migration is still seasonal.

	Southern Xinjiang	Northern Xinjiang	Eastern Xinjiang	Total
2000	1,573,834	5,448,476	467,609	7,489,919
2010	1,912,181	6,364,995	552,818	8,829,994

Figure 3. Han population numbers in 2000 and 2010 (based on Toops (2013, 19–21)).

	Southern Xinjiang	Northern Xinjiang	Eastern Xinjiang	Total
2000	6,831,691	1,037,941	476,170	8,345,802
2010	8,192,428	1,277,634	531,240	10,001,302

Figure 4. Uyghur population numbers in 2000 and 2010 (based on Toops (2013, 19–21)).

Because the Han migrated to, or were resettled in, Xinjiang for various reasons and at different periods, they are a highly diverse category. Differentiation vis-à-vis other Han is an important component of their identity processes. The main labels used by Han to identify themselves and other Han in Xinjiang are: Bingtuaners[5] (Bingtuande; Han employed by the Xinjiang Production and Construction Corps, in Chinese briefly 'Bingtuan'), Border Supporters (Zhibiande; Han resettled to support 'the construction of socialism' [shehuizhuyi jianshe] in border regions since the 1950s), Qualified Personnel (Rencai; skilled workers and university graduates), and Floating Population (Liudong Renkou) or Blind Flows (Mangmu Liudong; both referring to migration not organized by the state). Further, there are Great Famine Refugees who came to Xinjiang between 1959 and 1962, Educated Youth (Zhiqing; militant youth sent to Xinjiang 'to learn from the peasants' during the Cultural Revolution), Second Generation (Di'er Dai; Han born in Xinjiang from parents who settled in the region) and Profit-Driven Migrants (lit. 'those who come only for the money') – a general term for the economically motivated migrants since the 1990s (Joniak-Lüthi 2013).

In the present article I focus on yet another identity category which partially overlaps with some of the above labels: Han who self-identify as Xinjiangers (Xinjiangren), Locals (Bendide) and Genuine Xinjiang Locals (Lao Xinjiang). I refer to them jointly as 'Xinjiang Han'. The Xinjiang Han I discuss here were either born in Xinjiang or they became local through long-term residence, mostly more than twenty years. They regard Xinjiang as one of their home places (laojia, jiaxiang), often a primary one. Border Supporters, Qualified Personnel, Blind Flows, Famine Refuges who settled outside of Bingtuan farms, as well as their descendants, form the specific group of Xinjiang Han that I focus on in this article. The processes I describe here are not representative of the identity negotiations of Bingtuaners, as these mostly live in nearly mono-ethnic Bingtuan towns and farms. In the present article I also do not discuss the identity processes of mixed Han-Uyghur couples and their offspring, or inter-ethnic adoptions; these also differ from those of Xinjiang Han I explore here. Individuals I focus on are Han by minzu, speak fluent Chinese (in addition to varying degree of Uyghur), are not married to Uyghur and are mostly not Muslim. Nevertheless, they regard themselves as

Uyghurized (*Weizuhuade*). Because censuses do not classify Han according to self-identifications, even rough estimates of how many of the Han living in southern Xinjiang belong to this specific category are not possible. However, they are undoubtedly a minority. This article focuses on their identity negotiations and the ways in which they construct their regional belonging.

Identity processes of Xinjiang Han

Han-Uyghur boundary processes

By 2011 Ms Wang was a long-time resident of Aqsu. She arrived there in the early 1980s from Henan Province in eastern China with her father and became a successful businesswoman. In the year before my arrival she bought a house and some land in a Uyghur village outside of the town area. She had the old house torn down and built a new Uyghur-style house, very similar to all the other houses of her Uyghur neighbours. In the courtyard, she had a Uyghur-style grapevine-rack constructed by a Uyghur carpenter to shade it. On that day in early June, the eve of the Dragon Boat Festival, we spent an afternoon at her home, chatting with Uyghur and Han workers and eating mulberries offered by her Uyghur neighbour. Later on, we went to town to join a small banquet of Han businessmen and government officials who gathered to celebrate the festival. The banquet took place in a Han restaurant and different kinds of meat were served, including pork, even though not much of it was eaten. My neighbour at the table was Mr Fei, a Han government official from a neighbouring county. Mr Fei's parents came to Xinjiang as Border Supporters in 1956 and settled in Aqsu District where Mr Fei was born. Mr Fei called himself Local (Bendide; Tusheng Tuzhangde, lit. 'born and grown up locally') and spoke proudly of his proficiency in the Uyghur language. He claimed he was able to understand 80 per cent of the Uyghur spoken in Aqsu District. Other guests at the table also boasted their own language abilities and for a while conversation switched to Uyghur. After this performance, as if fearing I might confuse them for Uyghur, Mr Fei turned to me and said: 'The Han and Uyghur are very different.' He continued,

> Look at the architecture: Han like twisted roofs, Uyghur have a different style, they build flat-roof houses. Food is yet another difference. We local Han adopted many things from the Uyghur, we became Uyghurized (*women Weizu-huade*). We eat their mutton, but they still don't eat our pork (*women chi tamen de yangrou, keshi tamen haishi bu chi women de darou*).[6]

The Han at the table continued to discuss how Uyghurized they were, and, on the other hand, made sure that the boundary between 'the Han' and 'the Uyghur' as two contrasting categories remained in place. As the evening progressed and lots of alcohol was consumed, the banquet participants engaged in another kind of boundary performance. Now, ancestral home-place identities in inner China (*neidi, kouli*) were mobilized. While conversation at the table was up until now in standard Chinese, participants now switched to their native dialects from Sichuan, Shaanxi, Henan, and Gansu and gave examples of these to others. Individuals who shared a common native place became very cordial with each other, toasting each other and engaging in discussions about the characteristics they shared. Simultaneously, however, a boundary between Xinjiang Han and all other Han was reinforced. The Han at the table argued that they, as Xinjiang Han, clearly differed from other Han, even in their ancestral homes. Through interactions with minorities, but also as a result of their hard lives in this distant borderland, Xinjiang Han became different from other Han.

The experiences of that day reveal a number of simultaneously occurring identity processes. First, the acculturation and situational boundary blurring was seen in the Uyghur architecture of Ms Wang's house, in Uyghur language performances, and in the expression 'we became Uyghurized' used by Mr Fei. Even while they acknowledged this acculturation, the guests at the table simultaneously emphasized distinctions between Han and Uyghur *minzu*. This was reflected in Mr Fei's statement that 'Han and Uyghur are different', in the pork served that evening, in the mobilization of home-place identities and dialects, and also in the absence of any Uyghur guests at the table. Lastly, in order to emphasize their sense of belonging to the place, and position themselves vis-à-vis Han in inner China and vis-à-vis other Han in Xinjiang, they performed their identities as Locals and Xinjiangers.

While scholars in the field of ethnicity studies draw attention to situational nature of identities (Bentley 1987; Wallman 1983), in the case at hand, these Han at once blurred boundaries by incorporating Uyghur-ness into their Han identity, and reaffirmed these boundaries by emphasizing the distinctions between these two *minzu*. In a similar way, they represented themselves as genuinely Han and, at the same time, argued that they were different from all other Han because they had become similar to the Uyghur. Hence, they were 'Uyghurized' but definitely not Uyghur; they were Han but definitely unlike all other Han.

'Uyghurization' (*Weizuhua*), the process by which Han assume ethnic markers associated with the Uyghur, was described by Han informants as a process in which 'we became similar to them', 'we took things over from them', or 'we learned things from them'. 'Uyghurization' was most often associated with the assumption of some character traits associated with the Uyghur, such as hospitality and straightforwardness, and was performed through language, food, dancing, and the mixed-ethnic composition of networks of reciprocity.[7] These Han were happy to discuss the process of 'Uyghurization' among themselves, as were my Uyghur research participants. The Han who claimed they were 'Uyghurized' drew on it as a resource to establish themselves as 'genuine' Xinjiangers vis-à-vis other Han in Xinjiang, especially the recent Profit-Driven Migrants and Bingtuaners. Uyghur, on the other hand, were happy to point out that though Xinjiang in general was becoming an increasingly Han place, the Uyghur had succeeded in 'Uyghurizing' at least some of the settlers.

Language was among the most frequently discussed aspects of accultura- tion. My Uyghur acquaintances in Aqsu repeatedly commented with great dis- appointment on the unwillingness of most Han immigrants to learn Uyghur. Unsurprisingly, when Han were able to speak it, and when the language ability was coupled with other signs of 'Uyghurization', this had the power to tem- porarily blur the Han-Uyghur boundaries. A conversation with the family of Ayturan from Aqsu District is illustrative of the way this blurring occurs. Aytur- am's parents live in the countryside where Han constitute a clear minority of about 20 per cent. 'All these Han can speak Uyghur', the parents reported, 'they are like us. They came in the 1950s and 1960s to "support the border- land", their children were born here ... It is impossible to tell Han from Uyghur in the village. All Han speak fluent Uyghur and eat *halal* food. They have become "Uyghurized"'. Though ability to speak Uyghur is the clearest sign of 'Uyghurization', other forms of linguistic cross-pollination were also seen as evidence of it; for example, the use of the Xinjiang variety of the Chinese language which has absorbed some Uyghur words and Uyghur sen- tence intonation.

Changing eating habits, particularly abstention from pork consumption and developing a liking for *nan* – flat bread baked in earthen ovens, provide another narrative of acculturation. Interestingly, *nan* was far more often subject of the discussions among both Han and Uyghur than pork. Xin- jiang Han born outside of Xinjiang typically pointed out that at first they did not like it, but gradually got used to the taste. After many years in Xinjiang, they learnt to appreciate and love its taste and reported beneficial medicinal qualities. The importance of *nan* should not, of course, be exaggerated in terms of boundary blurring; Han do not become Uyghur through the con- sumption of *nan*. At the same time, the progression from initially disliking *nan*, to developing a taste for it, until one could not live without it, was used by a number of Han and Uyghur as a metaphor to describe the process of 'Uyghurization' and becoming Xinjiang Local. Some Han born outside of Xinjiang also described the process of 'Uyghurization' through changing taste preferences that shifted from liking spicy (*la*) to liking sour (*suan*), a taste generally associated with Uyghur cuisine.[8]

While the adoption of Uyghur things by the Han was generally seen in posi- tive terms, a number of my Uyghur informants resented it as a form of cultural appropriation. As Han adopt things from the Uyghur, they argued, these Uyghur things tend to become 'Xinjiang things'. Food is one domain where this appropriation occurs, as Uyghur dishes such as *polo* (pilaw with mutton) become 'Xinjiang dishes' (*Xinjiang tecan*). Uyghur dances, referred by a growing number of Han in and outside of Xinjiang as 'Xinjiang dances' (*Xinjiang wu*), is another. The statement of Ms Li from Ürümchi reveals how this appropriation happens,

> We Xinjiang Hanzu don't have any special dances. The only dance we have is this 1–2–3–4 'public square dance' (*guangchang wu*), not beautiful at all … But dancing has become a trait associated with Xinjiangers. In inner China people associate Xinjiang with Uyghur dances. When we go to inner China, everybody wants us to dance because this is something special about Xinjiangers. (Fieldwork interview, August 2015)

Some female Uyghur informants in particular felt that something they perceived as their own unique characteristic – namely the reported Uyghur ability to dance even before they can walk – was taken away from them, appropriated by Han and incorporated into 'Xinjiang identity'. Still, they were in a clear minority. Though Uyghur sometimes made fun of Han dancing Uyghur dances (for instance when Han men unknowingly incorporated 'female' moves in their dancing), this mockery was rather restrained. Though it was sometimes laughed at, or occasionally even slightly resented, Han learning to dance Uyghur dances was widely perceived as another positive element of 'Uyghurization'.

Dancing takes place every day in the early morning and early evening in Xinjiang parks and on public squares. Some Han women dress with particular care for these events, donning large earrings, long dresses, flowery blouses, and even Atlas-silk skirts and Uyghur *doppa* hats. This type of clothing, combined with an ability to dance Uyghur dances competently have interesting effects on Uyghur spectators. This is illustrated by the conversation I had with Uyghur men who had gathered at the public square in Aqsu in summer 2015 to watch the dancers and occasionally join in. That evening, one woman was dancing particularly gracefully. She wore large earrings, a colourful embroidered blouse and danced every dance, each with a different Uyghur man. As we were all watching, I asked the onlookers about her:

Agnieszka:	She dances beautifully, which *minzu* is she?
Uyghur men watching:	[after thinking and discussing] We don't know.
Elderly Uyghur man:	She is a different *minzu* (*yi zu*).
Agnieszka:	Different *minzu*? So she's not Uyghur?
Elderly Uygur man:	No, she's from here, from Aqsu.
Two Uyghur men:	[hesitating] She seems Han, doesn't she?
Agnieszka [addressing the woman in the break]:	You dance so beautifully. I was wondering which *minzu* are you?
The dancing woman:	I don't have a *minzu* (*meiyou minzu*). I'm from the '*minzu* of *minzu* unity' (*minzu tuanjie de minzu*).

This conversation is revealing in several ways. Firstly, it demonstrates that, although it might seem trivial, the ability to dance Uyghur dances competently and some knowledge of the Uyghur dress code can situationally confuse Han-Uyghur distinctions. Also, it made the men in the crowd reluctant to refer to the female dancer as 'Han', though it is likely that some of them knew this was her actual *minzu*. Also the dancing woman refused to identify as a particular *minzu* instead blurring the boundaries between them, as she danced Uyghur dances with Uyghur men. In this particular moment, she was both Han and Uyghur, and neither.

Dancing, professing a love for Uyghur cuisine, familiarity with the dress code, ability to communicate in Uyghur can all enable situational boundary blurring. At the same time, Xinjiang Han rarely convert to Islam and thus religion remains an unbridgeable divide which can call into question the notion of 'Uyghurization', since both parties are aware that the Han are unlikely to convert. However, it does not appear that the Uyghur actually expect Xinjiang Han, however acculturated they may be, to actually convert to Islam, except in cases of intermarriage or adoption. The situation of Han becoming Muslim was indeed too confusing to even imagine for many of the informants. They preferred instead to introduce a degree of porosity into the boundary between the two *minzu*, but to leave the boundary itself in place. Uyghur preferred Han to be *similar* to Uyghur in *some* respects, while at the same time certain distinctions, in particular religion, were maintained.

While this boundary blurring and self-proclaimed 'Uyghurization' might seem trivial to an outside observer and limited to superficial elements like language, dance, food, elements of house architecture or imaginary character traits, it is deeply significant for local Han and makes them feel that they 'belong' in Xinjiang. 'Uyghurization' and this feeling of belonging are central to the ways in which these Han regard themselves as superior to the more recent Han migrants to Xinjiang. It is also how they establish themselves as a distinct community vis-à-vis other Han in inner China.

Xinjiang Han vis-à-vis other Han

Research on home-place identities suggests that these are crucial to Han identity negotiations in inner China (Joniak-Lüthi 2015a). It is also reflected in identity processes of the Xinjiang Han. At the same time, in Xinjiang, the role of the ancestral home places appears less significant than in other parts of China. Though some Han mentioned them, very few thought that ties to these places had a determining influence on their everyday sociality, for example, on who their business partners were, or on the composition of their social networks. Since transportation in Xinjiang has become more efficient, some of my informants have visited their ancestral homes in eastern China, but in general they found no close family or friends there, and told me that they had no 'feeling' (*ganjue*) for it. Numerous Xinjiang Han also stressed they could not get used to the people, food, and climate in inner China. Mutton was tasteless and fruit were not sweet there, they said. In fact, families of Xinjiang Han frequently send Xinjiang fruit and *nan* to family members studying or working in eastern China to help them 'survive' away from home; a practice also common among the Uyghur. A number of my Han informants felt they did not belong in inner China and were not able to cope with how things were done there. Ms Zhang, for example, told me the following:

> I am Second Generation [her parents settled in Xinjiang], my husband is Fourth Generation [his great-grandparents settled in Xinjiang]. We have no other home than Xinjiang. When we go to inner China, we feel it's a different life, it's not our life […]. You see, we don't eat pork, we are used to eating noodles with mutton; we are used to the climate here. We have no other place where we belong. (Fieldwork interview, August 2015)

Mention of the absence of 'feeling' and family ties, difficulties in coping with the climate in inner China, individualization of the society there, the rapid pace of life and social pressure, the absence of familiar foods, and the omnipresence of pork were the main elements in a discourse which emphasized difference from inner China, and a feeling of not belonging there. The frequent discussions about how displaced Xinjiang Han felt in inner China, and the contrasting of Xinjiang Han and other Han, suggests that this distinction is crucial to their identity negotiations. Indeed, othering along this axis occurred just as often as the discussions of the complex boundary processes vis-à-vis the Uyghur.

Though Xinjiang Han do not doubt their own Han-ness, they differentiate between those Han living 'within the passes' (*kouli*), and those Han living 'outside of the passes' (*kouwai*), who are thus outside of the area regarded as the historic homeland of the Han/Chinese. Xinjiang's location 'outside of the passes' contributes the prevailing conception of Xinjiang as a backward (*luohou*) frontier, a place of opportunity but not suitable as somewhere to settle down (Joniak-Lüthi 2015b). At the same time, the 'backwardness' of Xinjiang, and thus by extension of Xinjiang Han, is also drawn on as a resource to construct Xinjiang Han as pure, unspoiled, honest, hospitable, straightforward, and laid-back, living in an unspoiled environment and consuming healthy food. This image is positively contrasted with social pressure, monetarization of relationships and the individualization of life in eastern China, even if this contrasting indirectly strips Xinjiang Han of the markers of Chinese modernity.

While othering of the Han 'within the passes' plays an important role in the formulation of collective subjectivity, othering of recent Han migrants to Xinjiang and migrant workers whose migration is disparaged as having a merely mercenary motivation – is just as important. My Uyghur informants also made this distinction, as illustrated by Mr Hamut, who told me,

> Han have unacceptable customs. They are dirty, make a lot of noise. [But] we can live with the early Han migrants, those who came long time ago or were born

and grew up here. They are very harmonious, they respect our customs. They respect us. We assimilated them, we protect them. New migrants are different [...] they only come here to earn money. They have no education and no culture. (Fieldwork interview, summer 2012)

Before the numbers of the Han in southern Xinjiang started to grow more rapidly in the 1990s, it appears that the acquisition of Uyghur language was quite common among Han settlers. While it is unlikely even then that all Han were able to speak it, many did so out of necessity in the course of their daily life. A significant number of my Han informants in Aqsu in their forties and fifties recalled that they were able to communicate in Uyghur when they were children but lost this ability in adult life as the need to speak Uyghur decreased. On the one hand, this is related to changes in language policy; on the other, it shows that at a certain moment the Han population in Aqsu reached a critical mass after which there was no need for Han to learn Uyghur anymore as all their needs could be satisfied without it. Today, Han can live very easily in southern Xinjiang towns without relying on Uyghur as providers of any services, except for baking *nan*.

Economic migration since the mid-1990s has transformed the linguistic situation, in particular because of the new forms that this migration has taken. Significantly, short-term and seasonal migration became possible during this period, owing to the greater convenience of travel within Xinjiang and between Xinjiang and inner China. Also, the end of the national work assignment system changed the way people migrated. While earlier migrants were forced to remain in Xinjiang for long periods of time because of the absence of transportation networks and the work assignment system, Profit-Driven Migrants since the 1990s are free to come and go as they please. Migration became more a temporary, market-dependent endeavour. This obviously decreases the time migrants are exposed to the Uyghur language and culture on their journeys between various temporary jobs in China and abroad. In comparison to these Han who come and go, the Xinjiang Han position themselves as Genuine Xinjiang Locals with the right to the place acquired through their efforts to become part of it.

For other Han the process of becoming a Xinjianger might comprise other elements than those described here. The Bingtuaners, for example, tend to construct their Xinjiang identity around the idea of the successful conquering of wasteland (*huangdi*) – referring to Xinjiang in the 1950s – which they turned into valuable, fertile land. Though the Bingtuan Han also adopted certain things from the Uyghur, such as food preferences, they rarely discuss these as examples of 'Uyghurization'. Instead, they are framed as the acquisition 'local characteristics' (*difang tedian*). Though these Han also use their Xinjiang Han identity to position themselves in relation to other Han and to the Uyghur, this identity is made of different elements which crucially affect how it is performed.

Conclusion

Xinjiang mass media frequently broadcast examples of Uyghur individuals learning from the Han or becoming like Han, such as success stories of Uyghur women who after education in eastern China challenge power hierarchies in their families. When I explained to my Uyghur and Han colleagues that I wanted to explore the contrary process, namely, of Han becoming like Uyghur, reactions were enthusiastic but simultaneously it was observed that it was a sensitive topic. To explore the processes of Uyghur assimilation is great, but to claim that the members of the national majority become 'minoritized' is taboo, in the words of my informants. Characterising dancing as an example of 'minzu unity' is what all newspapers do, but to discuss it as an aspect of 'Uyghurization' is something else. To praise Uyghur-speaking Han as those who make an effort to establish bridges between the minzu is fine, but to claim that it is a sign of acculturation which reveals the importance of the Uyghur language is not acceptable. The tendency to portray Uyghur dances and Uyghur food as 'Xinjiang dances' and 'Xinjiang specialties' reveals the reluctance on the part of many Han in Xinjiang to acknowledge that they have adopted certain things from their Uyghur 'other' and integrated them into their own identity, an identity which they now use to establish a boundary between themselves and other Han. The great majority of Xinjiang Han, unlike many other Han in Xinjiang, willingly discussed trans-minzu cultural borrowing and the situational blurring of minzu boundaries. However, although this blurring is socially significant, it has no influence on official minzu classification.

Minzu and ethnicity

When the Minzu Classification project was launched in the 1950s, its long-term implications could not have been predicted by project initiators. Research teams sent to multiethnic areas to identify the minzu and classify them with respect to their historical, cultural, social, and material 'advancement'[9] could not foresee how these minzu would behave sixty years later. They were conceived as stable categories to assure the smooth operation of bureaucratic power. Today, the official minzu status can be altered only through complex administrative procedures and with the consent of state institutions. The situational blurring of boundaries, acculturation, the multiple identities of one's offspring, or identity switching are all irrelevant to official classification.

In strict terms, ethnicity, understood as a process in which a boundary between 'us' and 'them' is established for the purpose of identification and organization (Barth [1969] 1996), a process that occurs under an eye of the state (Barth 1994) and the market (Comaroff and Comaroff 2009), has little in common with *minzu*. Boundary making and maintenance, crucial to ethnicity, are hardly relevant to the state-established categories of *minzu*. While ethnicity can be practiced in a non-exclusive and situational manner (while restricted by its relational quality), *minzu* status is not negotiable. Despite these differences, however, there appear some important parallels. As with ethnicity which, especially in times of mobilization, tends to employ essentialist discourses of shared culture, shared blood, common origin, and history (Barth [1969] 1996; Eriksen 2002; Jenkins 1997), *minzu* were constructed as historically formed communities of shared culture, language and economy, following Stalin's definition of nationality (1950 (II), 268–272). Moreover, the role of *minzu* subjectivities today far exceeds the control of state agencies, and has moved far beyond the original administrative role intended for *minzu* classification.

Depending on how they were classified in terms of their social advancement, minority *minzu* have been able to profit from a number of affirmative action policies, such as extra points in university entry exams, the legal right to have more than one child, or the *nominal* right to education and media in their mother tongue.[10] At the same time, however, minorities have had to live with disempowerment, infantilization of their cultures, as well as forced assimilation, and other examples of the power inequality which has been institutionalized through the *minzu* classification which distinguishes between the 'advanced' Han majority and minorities who are expected to 'catch up'. Both the affirmative action policies and the discrimination have made minority *minzu* labels socially important in a way which is today lamented by some as a threat to the unity of the Chinese nation (Ma 2014). Some *minzu* have indeed become brands in the identity economy (Comaroff and Comaroff 2009). The Uyghur *minzu* was created during the Minzu Classification project out of a number of locally significant ethnic varieties and thus the Uyghur 'brand' has been crucial in the establishment of contemporary Uyghur subjectivity. At the same time, since its official recognition, the Uyghur *minzu* has 'ethnicized' and has assumed a potency which the Chinese state finds hard to manage today.

On the one hand, the Uyghur and the Han are two *minzu* which are constructed in formal, administrative terms as stable, mutually exclusive and impenetrable categories. On the other hand, people classified as Uyghur and Han are linked by a relationship of differentiation whose history predates the Communist-era, or even Republican-era classifications. At the turn of the twentieth century, the differentiation between Han and Uyghur, or in the contemporary nomenclature between Khitay, Kafir and Khaqanī and, on the other hand, Chantou, Turki, and Musulman already existed, even though in southern Xinjiang the othering along this axis was much less central to identity negotiations than today.[11] In other areas and communities in China, it is possible that *minzu* classification affected social practice to a lesser extent, especially where it did not follow locally significant collective subjectivities. The *minzu* boundary between Han and Uyghur, however, did merge partially with earlier modes of differentiation; it reinforced and institutionalized them. Hence, today Han and Uyghur in Xinjiang interact in two dimensions: as members of two *minzu* constructed and administered by the state, and as members of two ethnicities. While in *minzu* classification it is only possible to be officially either Han or Uyghur, in the mundane processes of ethnicity, situational boundary blurring does occur. This demonstrates that state-enforced categories of identity may become ethnic and assume functions not foreseen, or granted, by the state. Thus, though the role of the Chinese state is inherent in the processes of ethnicity, since it officially recognizes some categories of identity and ignores others, the way the state-established categories are 'ethnicized' ultimately eludes the control of the state.

Notes

1. But see Lattimore (1932), Hansen (2005), Blum (2001), Cliff (2012), Li (2010) and Vasantkumar (2012).
2. I use the Uyghur Computer Alphabet to transliterate Uyghur words in this article, except for some toponyms like Kashgar and Hotan, where pre-existing forms of transliteration are better known to English-language speakers. Pinyin Romanization is used for Chinese.
3. The semantic fields of these two names were largely synonymous prior to 1949. That is why I decided on to use this term.
4. Zhou (1990, 283), Li and Yang (1994, 28), RPB (2012) and Toops (2013, 19–22).
5. Bingtuan is a Han-dominated organization under the direct jurisdiction of the central government. See Becquelin (2004) and Cliff (2009).
6. On boundary processes between Han and Uyghur in Xinjiang see, for example, Smith (2002), Li (2010) and Caprioni (2011).
7. Compare Li (1998).
8. At the same time, though Xinjiang Han emphasize they can cook and love to eat Uyghur dishes, some also stress that Han cook these dishes differently. For *polo* (rice with mutton), for example, leaner meat is cut into smaller chunks, and better-quality oil is used, my Han informants argued. It is also never consumed using hands, as it sometimes is in Uyghur homes.
9. This advancement was measured against the evolutionist scales of Josef Stalin and Lewis H. Morgan. For details, see Joniak-Lüthi 2015a.
10. The Han, as the most advanced *minzu*, are not officially eligible for affirmative action policies, but in practice, depending on their household registration (e.g. rural, in a border area), they profit from these policies in a similar way to the minority *minzu*.
11. Eric Schluessel (personal communication, February 2015).

Acknowledgements

The first draft of this paper was presented at the annual meeting of the Association for Asian Studies in Philadelphia in 2014. I would like to thank my co-panelists Cheng

Yinghong, Dru Gladney and Mao Yufeng, and our audience, for their feedback. Further, I thank the editor and the four anonymous referees of the journal for their very helpful comments. Last, I own greatest debt to my research partners and research participants in Xinjiang. They, unfortunately, have to remain anonymous.

Disclosure statement

No potential conflict of interest was reported by the authors.

Funding

I am grateful to the Swiss National Science Foundation, UniBern Research Foundation, and the German Ministry for Education and Research (collective grant for the network Crossroads Asia) for funding the research on which this article is based.

References

Akesu Diqu Tongjiju, ed. 2011. "Akesu diqu 2010 diliuci quanguo renkou pucha zhuyao shuju gongbao (1)." [Major Results of the Sixth National Population Census 2010 for Aqsu District, No 1]. http://wenku.baidu.com.

Barth, Fredrik. ([1969] 1996). "Ethnic Groups and Boundaries." In *Theories of Ethnicity: A Classical Reader*, edited by Werner Sollors, 294–324. Houndmills: Macmillan Press.

Barth, Fredrik. 1994. "Enduring and Emerging Issues in the Analysis of Ethnicity." In *The Anthropology of Ethnicity: Beyond 'Ethnic Groups and Boundaries'*, edited by Hans Vermeulen and Cora Govers, 11–32. Amsterdam: Het Spinhuis.

Becquelin, Nicolas. 2004. "Staged Development in Xinjiang." *The China Quarterly* 178: 358–378.

Bentley, G. Carter. 1987. "Ethnicity and Practice." *Comparative Studies in Society and History* 29 (1): 24–55.

Blum, Susam D. 2001. *Portaits of "Primitives": Ordering Human Kinds in the Chinese Nation*. Lanham: Rowman and Littlefield Publishers.

Caprioni, Elena. 2011. "Daily Encounters Between Hans and Uyghurs in Xinjiang: Sinicization, Integration or Segregation." *Pacific Affairs* 84 (2): 267–287.

Chu, Yiting. n.d. "The Power of Knowledge: A Critical Analysis of the Depiction of Ethnic Minorities in China's Elementary Textbooks." Unpublished paper.

Cliff, Thomas. 2009. "Neo Oasis: The Xinjiang *Bingtuan* in the Twenty-First Century." *Asian Studies Review* 33 (1): 83–106.

Cliff, Thomas. 2012. "The Partnership of Stability in Xinjiang: State-Society Interactions Following the July 2009 Unrest." *The China Journal* 68: 79–105.

Comaroff, John L., and Jean Comaroff. 2009. *Ethnicity, Inc.* Chicago, IL: Chicago University Press.

Eriksen, Thomas Hylland. 2002. *Ethnicity and Nationalism: Anthropological Perspectives*. London: Pluto Press.

Fei, Hsiao-tung. 1980. "Ethnic Classification in China." *Social Science in China* 1: 94–107.

Gladney, Dru C. 1994. "Representing Nationality in China: Refiguring Majority/Minority Identities." *The Journal of Asian Studies* 53 (1): 92–123.

Gladney, Dru C. 1998. *Ethnic Identity in China: The Making of a Muslim Minority Nationality (Case Studies in Cultural Anthropology)*. Fort Worth, TX: Harcourt Brace College Publishers.

Hansen, Mette Halskov. 2005. *Frontier People: Han Settlers in Minority Areas of China.* London: Hurst and Company.

Jenkins, Richard. 1997. *Rethinking Ethnicity: Arguments and Explorations.* London: Sage Publications.

Joniak-Lüthi, Agnieszka. 2013. "Han Migration to Xinjiang Uyghur Autonomous Region: Between State Schemes and Migrants' Strategies." *Zeitschrift für Ethnologie* 138: 155–74.

Joniak-Lüthi, Agnieszka. 2015a. *The Han: China's Diverse Majority.* Seattle: University of Washington Press.

Joniak-Lüthi, Agnieszka. 2015b. "Xinjiang's Geographies in Motion." *Asian Ethnicity* 16 (4): 428–445.

Lattimore, Owen. 1932. "Chinese Colonization in Manchuria." *The Geographical Review* 22 (2): 177–95.

Li, Xiaoxia. 1998. "Lun Xinjiang Hanzu Difang Wenhua de Xingcheng ji Qi Tezheng [Local Culture of Xinjiang Hanzu: Process of Formation and its Characteristics]." *Minzu Yanjiu (Nationality Studies)* 3: 39–44.

Li, Jie. 2010. *Xinjiang nanjiang diqu Hanzu yimin ji minzu guanxi yanjiu - Yi Akesu diqu Baicheng xian nongcun Hanzu yimin ji minzu guanxi wei li [A Study of Han Migration and Inter-Ethnic Relations in Southern Xinjiang: Rural Han Immigrants and Inter-Ethnic Relations in Bai County in Aqsu District].* Beijing: Minzu Chubanshe.

Li, Jianxin, and Limin Yang. 1994. "Xinjiang liangci renkou pucha jan renkou chushenglü biandong chengyin ji renkou kongzhi xiaoguo pingjia [The Assessment of the Changing Birth Rates and Efficacy of Population Control in the Time Between Two Censuses]." *Xibei Renkou Yanjiu (Northwestern Population Studies)* 55: 28–32.

Ma, Rong. 2014. "Reflections on the Debate on China's Ethnic Policy: My Reform Proposals and their Critics." *Asian Ethnicity* 15 (2): 237–246.

Mullaney, Thomas S. 2011. *Coming to Terms with the Nation: Ethnic Classification in Modern China.* Berkeley, CA: University of California Press.

RPB (Renkou Pucha Bangongshi), Guojia Tongjiju and Renkou he Jiuye Tongjisi, eds. 2012. *Zhongguo 2010 nian renkou pucha ziliao [2010 Population Census Tabulation].* Beijing (electronic version).

Smith, Joanne N. 2002. "'Making Culture Matter': Symbolic, Spatial and Social Boundaries between Uyghurs and Han Chinese." *Asian Ethnicity* 3 (2): 153–174.

Stalin, Joseph W. 1950. *Werke.* Band II: 1907–1913. Berlin: Dietz Verlag.

Toops, Stanley. 2013. "Spatial Results of the 2010 Census of Xinjiang." The annual meeting of the Association of Asian Studies, San Diego, March 21–24.

Vasantkumar, Chris. 2012. "Han at Minzu's Edges: What Critical Han Studies Can Learn from China's 'Little Tibet'." In *Critical Han Studies: The History, Representation, and Identity of China's Majority,* edited by Thomas S. Mullaney, James Leibold, Stéphane Gros, and Eric Vanden Bussche, 234–55. Berkeley, CA: Global, Area, and International Archive and University of California Press.

Wallman, Sandra. 1983. "Identity Options." In *Minorities: Community and Identity,* edited by Charles Fried, 69–78. Berlin: Springer-Verlag.

XWZCZ (Xinjiang Weiwu'er Zizhiqu Chengli 50 Zhounian Chouweihui Bangongshi) and Xinjiang Weiwu'er Zizhiqu Tongjiju, eds. 2005. *Xinjiang wushi nian 1955–2005 [Xinjiang: Fifty Years 1955–2005].* Beijing: Zhongguo Tongji Chubanshe.

Zhou, Chongjing. 1990. *Zhongguo renkou, Xinjiang fence [China's Population, Xinjiang Volume].* Beijing: Zhongguo Caizheng Jingji Chubanshe.

Index

Note: Page numbers in **bold** type refer to figures
Page numbers in *italic* type refer to tables
Page numbers followed by 'n' refer to notes

Abilov, B. 65
Adler, A., Marmot, N. and Sing-Manoux, A. 92
affirmative action policies 123
African-American labour 82
African-Americans 94
agricultural communities 7
Al Azhar University (Egypt) 35, 36
alien cultural others 26
Almaty (Kazakhstan) 54
America *see* United States of America (USA)
Americans, Chinese 73
ancestral home-place identities 116, 119
Angola 79
Aqsu District 111, *112*, 117
Aqsu (Xinjiang) 112, 117; businesswoman 115
artefacts, ethnic 21
Asad, T. 26
assimilation (forced) 123
attainment: educational 99, 102, 103, *see also* socioeconomic attainment
Auezov, M. 64, 65
Australian media 73
autonomous ethnic regions 16, 96, 97
availability heuristic 94

Barabantseva, E. 32
Bennett, T., and Savage, M. 93
Bian, Y., Davis, D. and Wang, S. 93
Bingtuan Han 121
Bingtuaners 114, 121, 124n5
Blind Flows 114
Bonacich, E. 78, 79
Border Supporters 114, 115

boundaries and subjectivities 109–24; Han and Uyghur in Xinjiang 112–15; interviews 111–12, 118, 120–1, 122; population numbers 113, **113**, **114**; Xinjiang Han *vis-à-vis* other Han 119–21
Bourdieu, P. 93
British elites 82
Bryman, A. 41
Burkhanov, A., and Chen, Y.-W. 9–10, 51–70

California food industry 78
call centres 78–9
Cantonese script 4
Cantonese speakers 6
capital, cultural 93
casual racism 77
CCP (Chinese Communist Party) 16, 21, 25, 95
Census: (China, 2000) 8; (China, 2010) 94–5, 113
Central Asia policy 52
Central Asian populace 51
Central Plains agricultural communities 7
centrally planned economy 17
Centres, R. 104
Chambishi Mine 83
Chen, Y.-W., and Burkhanov, A. 9–10, 51–70
Chicago 73
China, territorial claims 43–4
China Islamic Association 36
Chinatowns, Europe 7
Chinese Communist Party (CCP) 16, 21, 25, 95

Chinese employers 10
Chinese genealogy 26
Chinese Historical Museum 21
Chinese languages 40, 100, 113, 116
Chinese Revolutionary Museum 21
Chongqing 63
Christian minorities 6
citizenship: Malaysian 40, 43; PRC 31
class: culturalist 93, 103; hierarchies 93;
     identification 92–4, 102, *102, 103*;
     identity 95–7; perceptions 104;
     self-placement 104; social 93;
     subjective 92, 97, 98; subjectivity 104;
     underclass formation 73; upper 98
Clinton, W. (Bill) 73
clothing, in Xinjiang 118–19
Collum Coal Mine 76, 84
common history myth 22
Communist Party: Chinese (CCP) 16, 21,
     25, 95; propaganda 56
Communist revolution 23, 25
Concise History of the She Nationality, The
     (Bianxiezu) 23
consciousness, ethnic 95
Constitution of Kazakhstan 57
convenience sampling 41
corporations, Chinese 63
cosmopolitans 58
CPN (Cultural Palace of Nationalities) 18,
     19, 20–1, *20, 21*
cultural capital 93
cultural Chinese identity 40
cultural differences 23
cultural entrepreneurs 39
cultural inventions 17
Cultural Palace of Nationalities (CPN) 18,
     19, 20–1, *20, 21*
cultural participation 100
cultural particularities 22
cultural production 15
cultural representation 14
Cultural Revolution 95
culturalist class analysis 93, 103
culture: and education 40–1; ethnic
     minority 6–7; highbrow 100; Uyghur
     100
cut flower industry 78

dances 118–19, 122
Danforth, L.M. 35, 47
Davis, D., Bian, Y. and Wang, S. 93
Davis, N., and Robinson, R. 98
day labourers, Latino 78
Dharamsala Tibetan community 4
diaspora, overseas Chinese 9, 65

dietary restrictions, religious 73, 115,
     117–18, 119, 120, 122
differences: cultural 23; religious 5–6
Dillon, M. 1–12
discursive marginalization 78
diversity 52
domestic workers, Latina 73
dress code, in Xinjiang 118–19
Dungans 33
Dutch East India Company 2

eating habits 73, 115, 117–18, 119, 120,
     122
economy, centrally planned 17
Educated Youth 114
education and culture 40–1
educational attainment 99, 102, 103
egalitarian behaviour 77
Egemen Qazaqstan 62, 63
Egypt, Al Azhar University 35, 36
elites 75, 82; ruling 53, 67n2
employees and employers in Africa 10,
     71–84; African women workers 82–3;
     African/Chinese interface 74–7;
     concept of racialization 72–3, 77–9;
     integration and segregation 80–2;
     interviews 72, 84n1; poor conditions
     74–5, 76; South-South labour
     racialization 79–83; work conditions
     74–5
Engels, F., and Marx, K. 92
entrepreneurs 39
equality 20
Equatorial Guinea 80
ethnic artefacts 21
ethnic autonomous areas 2
ethnic Chinese label 46
ethnic classifiers 15
ethnic consciousness 95
ethnic identification campaign 27
ethnic identity (*minzu*) 25, 95–7, 122,
     123–4
ethnic inequalities 96
ethnic minorities 110–11
ethnic minority culture 6–7
ethnic pride 47
ethnic representation 13–27; constructed
     hierarchical brotherhood 22–6;
     national minorities 17–21; scientific
     knowledge production 15–17
ethnic tourism 22
ethnical diversity 52
ethnicity, Hui 31
ethnicization process 33
ethnonationalists 58–9

Europe, Chinatowns 7
European identity and Muslims 26
Evans, M.D.R., and Kelley, J. 92, 94, 104
EXPO-2017 61, 64
extremists, Uyghurs 95

Falungong 6
familiar stranger description 47
Fan, K. 8–9, 11, 13–29
feudal serfdom 24
Floating Population 114
food 117; industry 78; Uyghurs 119
foreign policy 52, 53
Foucault, M. 17
Freedom House 77
Fujian Provincial Archive (FPA) 18, 19, 22

gang-related incidents 73
Genuine Xinjiang Locals 114, 117
Ghanaian employees 77
Gillner, B. 57
Gini coefficient 96
Gladney, D.C. 33–4, 47
Global North enterprises 72
globalization factors 34
Gombak (Selangor, Malaysia) 37
government policy 6
Great Famine Refugees 114
Great Hall of the People's Congress 18
Great Leap Forward 17
Great Western Development campaign
    95
Gunn, S. 93

Hakka community 3
halal food 117
Hall, S. 14
Han: advanced people 25, 96; chauvinism
    25; government official 115;
    population (Aqsu District) **112**;
    settlement Xinjiang 113; in Uyghur
    112–15; Xinjiang Han vis-à-vis other
    Han 119–21
Han Chinese Muslims 42
Han Chinese traders 113, 124n3
Han dynasty 7
Hanren (people of Han) 7
health care reform, USA 73
Herzfeld, M. 25
hierarchical evolutionary structure 23–4
highbrow culture 100
Ho, W.Y. 30
Hodge, R.W., and Treiman, D. 92
home-place identities, ancestral 116, 119
Hong Kong 4

Hu Jintao 75
Hunt, M., and Ray, R. 92

identification and self-identification
    10–11
identity: ancestral home-place 116, 119;
    construction 34–5, 116; cultural
    Chinese 40; economy 123; ethnic
    (minzu) 95–7, 122, 123–4; ethnic
    Uyghur 10–11, 91, 100, 102, 104,
    112–13; Hui 33; Islamic 98; Muslim
    Chinese 30–48; national 3; political and
    national 42; transnational 32; Xinjiang
    118
illegal migration 65
immigrant workers: biases against 73;
    racist phrases about 74, see also
    employees and employers in Africa
income 79–80
India: call centres 78–9; comparison with
    China 2
industrial production facilities 63
inequalities 96
Institutional of Islamic Thought and
    Civilization (ISTAC) 40
integration 80–2
intellectuals 105
intelligentsia, Kazakh-speaking 57
interethnic equality 20
interethnic relations 23
International Islamic University (UIA) 36,
    37, 40
internationalism, Islamic 34
inventions, cultural 17
Islam 99, 119, see also Muslim Chinese
    identities
Islamic identity 98
Islamic Umma 113
Israeli, R. 34
ISTAC (Institutional of Islamic Thought
    and Civilization) 40

Jackman, M. 92, 98; and Jackman, R. 94
Jingpo people 18–19, 24
Joniak-Lüthi, A. 11, 109–26
jujube plantations 113

Karavan 57
Kazakhstanskaia Pravda 60–1, 62–3
Kelley, J., and Evans, M.D.R. 92, 94, 104
Khorgos 62
Kinshasa Chinese community 80
kinship metaphors 25
knowledge, Islamic 42, 44
Kristenson, M., and Lundberg, J. 92

Kunming railway station 112

labour marker discrimination 96
labour standards *see* employees and
    employers in Africa
Laclau, E., and Mouffe, C. 59
Laitin, D.D. 39, 46
Land Reform 24
languages: Chinese 6, 40, 100, 113, 116;
    Kazakhstan 58, 59, 60, 66; and
    representation 14; Romance 4; Russian
    56; spoken 4, 12n3; Turkic 113;
    Uyghur 96, 100, 113, 115, 116, 121;
    written 3–4
Laruelle, M., and Peyrouse S. 51
Latina domestic workers 73
Latino day labourers 78
Lawler, S. 93
legitimacy, nationality 26
Lindemann, K. 92
Lipman, J.N. 33
living standards 95
Locals 114, 115
Lonmin mine 76
Los Angeles 73
Luanshya Copper Mine (LCM) 81–2
Lundberg, J., and Kristenson, M. 92

Ma, H., and Ngeow C.B. (Peter) 9, 30–50
Macedonians 35
magazines 55
majority nationalities 109
Malay Muslims 9, 73
Malaysia: Chinese minority tensions 73;
    Chinese-language schools 40; Muslims
    9; non-Muslim Chinese 46; political
    system 42
Malaysia-China Muslim Chamber of
    Commerce 38
Malaysian citizenship 40, 43
Manchuria 8
Mandarin 4
manufacturing 80
marginalization, discursive 78
market reforms 96
Marmot, N., Adler, A. and Sing-Manoux, A.
    92
Marx, K. 92; and Engels, F. 92
Marxist social development model 23
mass media 122
Massimov, K. 63
Mecca 95
media 73; African refuges 73; funding 56,
    67n3; mass 122; as sources of
    discourses 55–6; Soviet press 55–6;

state-owned 55; Xinjiang 122, *see also*
    newspaper study
metaphors, kinship 25
Mexican-Americans 72–3
migrants: New Commonwealth 72;
    profit-driven 114, 121; and tourists 64–6
migration: Chinese 64–6; illegal 65
Miles, R. 72
mines in Zambia 76, 77, 79, 81–2, 83, 84
minorities: Muslim 30; national 16, 122
minority group membership 21
minority nationalities 109
minzu (ethnic identity) classification 25
mobility, upward 95
monoculture 1
Mouffe, C., and Laclau, E. 59
museums, ethnic artefacts 21
music appreciation 100
Muslim Chinese identities 30–48;
    accommodation and separatism 33–4;
    community formation 36–7; education
    abroad 35–6; interviews 38–41; Muslim
    students survey 41–4, *42*, *43*, *44*;
    overseas minorities 32–3, 48n1;
    political and national identity *45*;
    theoretical discussion 44–8; and
    transnationalism 34–5
Muslim communities 5–6
Muslim minorities 30
Muslim region 112
Muslim students 35–6, 41–4; survey 41–4,
    42, *43*, *44*
Muslims: and European identity 26; Han
    Chinese 42; Hui 31; Malay 9, 73; Uyghur
    31

nan (flat bread) 117, 121
narrating historiography 21
nation-building 9, 25
National Days 18, 21
National Hui Conference (Quanzhou,
    2012) 38
national identity 3
national minorities 16, 122
national policy 20
national solidarity 13
nationalist activities, Uyghur 93
nationalist groups, Kazakh 58
nationality: legitimacy 26; Stalin's
    definition 123
Nazarbayev, N. 61
New Commonwealth migrants 72
newspaper reading 100
newspaper study 10, 51–67; Chinese
    tourists and migrants 64–6; direct

impact issues 66, 68n4; economic cooperation with China 62–3; empirical findings and discussions 59–60, *60*, 66; media as sources of discourses 55–6; newspapers studied and their readers 56–9; political cooperation with China 60–2; ruling elites 53, 67n2; Sino–Kazakhstani relations 52–5
Ngeow C.B. (Peter), and Ma, H. 9, 30–50
non-whites, racializing 79

Obama, B. 73
occupation, and social class 93
occupational attainment 93, 99
Office for the Celebration of National Day 21
One Belt One Road 30–1, 38, 52, 59, 63, 67n1
oppressed minorities 6
others, alien cultural 26
overseas Chinese diaspora 9, 65
Overseas Chinese Muslim Association (OCMA) 31, 37–8, 46, 47

People's Representative Congresses 16
People's Republic of China (PRC): citizenship 31; establishment 9; spokesperson for the people 14; ten-year anniversaries 18
Peyrouse S., and Laruelle, M. 51
piety 98–9
pilgrimages to Mecca 95
plantations 113
political and national identity 42
population categories 110
pork 73, 115, 116, 117, 120
post-Soviet states 51
primitive society 24
printed media *see* newspaper study
productivity differential studies 78
profit-driven migrants 114, 121
provincial origin 42, *43*
psychological abuse 24

Qing dynasty 7
Qiushu (Zhang) 7
qualified personnel 114

race-labour hierarchy, US 78, 82
racism 77
radio stations 55
Rahman, T.A. 36
Ray, R., and Hunt, M. 92
reading: ability 100, 101; newspapers 100
reference group theory 94

Referential Outline of the She Nationality Investigation (FPA) 22–3
refugees 114; African 73
Regional Islamic Da'wah Council of Southeast Asia and the Pacific (RISEAP) 36
religiosity 44, 98–9, 103–4, 119
religious dietary restrictions 73, 115, 117–18, 119, 120, 122
religious differences 5–6
religious piety 98–9
rhetorical racialization 84
Robinson, R., and Davis, N. 98
Romance languages 4
Rudelson, J. 92
Russian-language newspapers 56

Sagintayev, B. 65
Sakslind, R., and Skarpenes, O. 93
Sarkozy, N. 74
Sarym, A. 64
Sata, M. 84
Sautmann, B., and Yan, H. 10, 71–90
Savage, M., and Bennett, T. 93
Scott, G. 75
script 3–4
seafarers 78, 82
Second Generation 114, 120
self-identification and identification 10–11
Shanghai Cooperation Organization 52
She people 22–3; revolutionary history 23
Shoprite 77
Silk Road Economic Belt 30–1, 38, 52, 59, 63, 67n1
Sing-Manoux, A., Adler, A. and Marmot, N. 92
Sinocentrism 100
Sinophobia 10
Skarpenes, O., and Sakslind, R. 93
slave society 24
social advancement 123
social class and occupation 93
social development: Marxist model 23; models 24–5
social dynamics 110
social engineering projects 110
social stratification 93
socioeconomic attainment 91–104; class identification 92–4, 102, *102*, *103*; ethnic identity and class identity 95–7; respondents 101, *101*; study data 97–100; study findings 101–4; summary and discussions 104–5; Uyghurs in Xinjiang 94–5

solidarity, national 13
South Africa: manufacturing 80; police 76
Soviet press 55–6
spoken languages 4, 12n3
Standard Chinese 6
Stark, R. 98
State Council 19
state owned media 55
state sector jobs 96
status, urban 99–100
stereotypes 1, 15
stigmatization 19
Subei people 8
subjective class status 92, 97, 98
subjectivity: class 104, see also boundaries and subjectivities
Sudan 81, 83
Swokupmund (Namibia) 81
Syroezhkin, K. 54, 66

Tang dynasty 7
Tangren (people of Tang) 7
television stations 55
Tibet 4–5
Tibetan community Dharamsala 4
Tibetan independence 4
Tibetan society 24
tortilla industry 78
tourism 22
tourists 64–6
traders: Chinese 77; Han Chinese 113, 124n3
transnational identities 32
transnationalism 34–5
transport networks 121
Treiman, D., and Hodge, R.W. 92
Turkic language 113

UIA (International Islamic University) 36, 37, 40
underclass formation 73
uniformity myth 1, 3
United Nations (UN) 3
United States of America (USA): California food industry 78; health care reform 73; Los Angeles 73; race-labour hierarchy 78, 82
upper class 98
upward mobility 95
urban status 99–100

Ürümchi (Xinjiang) 97, 105, 111; riot (2009) 112; Uyghurs 11
Uyghurization 116–17, 118, 121
Uyghurized Han 11, 115, 116–17
Uyghurs 31, 33; architecture 116; cuisine 119; culture 100; dances 118–19, 122; dress code 118–19; ethnic identity 10–11, 91, 100, 102, 104, 112–13; extremists 95; intellectuals 105; language 96, 100, 113, 115, 116, 121; Muslims 31; nationalist activities 93; in Xinjiang 94–5, 112–15

Vasantkumar, C. 32
visa application 64–5
Vremia 57, 64

Wade, N. 74
wages 79–80
walnut plantations 113
Wang, S., Davis, D. and Bian, Y. 93
Wang, Y., and Yamaguchi, K. 92, 98
women workers, African 82–3
Wong, D. 33
work: assignment systems 121; conditions 74–5; ethic 79, 84n2; intensity comparative 74; suitability 78
workers: immigrant 73, 74, see also employees and employers in Africa
workplaces, good 102, 103
World Uyghur Congress 93
written languages 3–4

Xi Jingping 59–60, 61
Xinjiang: autonomous ethnic region 96; Chinese Communist Party (CCP) 95; conflict 4, 12n4; Uyghurs in 94–5
Xinjiang Uyghur Autonomous Region 10–11

Yamaguchi, K., and Wang, Y. 92, 98
Yan, H., and Sautmann, B. 10, 71–90
Yellow Emperor 7
Yi people 24
Yiwu (Zhejiang) 38

Zambia: mines 76, 77, 79, 81, 83, 84; political forces 75; textile factory 74
Zang, X. 10–11, 91–108
Zhas Alash 60, 61–2, 64, 65
zhiguo (backward) 24